The Sustainable Portfolio

Financial Planning for the Conscious Investor

By
Nathan Venture, D

The Sustainable Portfolio

Financial Planning for the Conscious Investor

Table of Contents

Aligning Your Values
with Your Financial Goals

Financial planning is often seen as a purely analytical task, filled with numbers, projections, and spreadsheets. But at its core, it is profoundly personal, shaped by the unique values and aspirations that each of us holds dear. Whether you're a young professional just starting out, a seasoned entrepreneur, or someone planning for retirement, your financial objectives are a reflection of what you value most in life. This introduction serves as a compass, aiming to guide you through a thoughtful alignment of your financial goals with your core values.

Consider for a moment what matters most to you. Is it security, freedom, family, or perhaps giving back to community causes? Aligning financial goals with these personal values isn't just a philosophical exercise; it's a strategic approach that can provide clarity and motivation, transforming the way you manage and grow your wealth. The good news is that achieving financial success and staying true to your principles aren't mutually exclusive paths. In fact, when these paths intersect, they create a roadmap that directs you toward a meaningful and fulfilling life.

Setting financial goals often starts with introspection—a deep dive into understanding the "why" behind your monetary objectives. This process requires you to question old habits, examine existing biases, and perhaps redefine what success actually means to you. The convergence of your financial and personal values forms a powerful narrative, allowing each financial decision to act as a stepping stone towards realizing your bigger life picture.

However, introducing values into financial planning isn't without its complexities. It demands that you face trade-offs and dilemmas. For instance, pursuing an entrepreneurial venture may align with your value of autonomy but might conflict with your financial security. This is where strategic planning and clear prioritization come into play. By identifying which values are most important, you make informed decisions that might even challenge conventional wisdom.

One effective method is to articulate your values into concise, clear statements. Once crafted, these statements don't just sit on paper; they act as guiding principles in every financial decision, from choosing investments to budgeting day-to-day expenses. For example, if environmental stewardship is a core value, integrating sustainable investments into your portfolio may not just be advantageous; it becomes imperative. This is where sustainable and socially responsible investing comes into play, aligning your financial goals with the broader impact you wish to have on the world.

Not surprisingly, the intersection of values and financial goals often brings a sense of peace and fulfillment. A values-centered approach allows individuals to invest with intention. This means every dollar spent or saved echoes your core beliefs, leading to a heightened sense of personal satisfaction—knowing that your money is doing good, not only for you but for others as well.

Values alignment serves as a powerful anchor in volatile markets. When prices fluctuate and uncertainty looms, having a value-based framework offers a stable reference point. This drives resilience in investment strategies, helping you to remain focused and committed rather than swayed by short-term temptations or market noise. Furthermore, it encourages a disciplined approach to wealth management, empowering you to stay the course and avoid impulsive decisions that may undermine long-term goals.

It's important to recognize that the journey of aligning values with financial goals has its own learning curve. It involves constant evaluation and recalibration. Life's circumstances change, as do our values. Regularly revisiting and reassessing your values and financial goals ensures they remain in harmony, adjusting as necessary to stay aligned with your evolving outlook.

For financial advisors, wealth managers, and educational professionals, embracing a values-centered approach offers an opportunity to forge deeper connections with clients and students. By incorporating values into the conversation, professionals can offer more personalized guidance and support, fostering long-term relationships built on trust and understanding. This client-focused approach becomes an invaluable service, particularly as more individuals seek financial partners who understand their unique aspirations and values.

Finally, the ripple effects of aligning values with financial objectives extend beyond individuals; they influence families, communities, and future generations. Parents who integrate values in their financial strategy not only benefit themselves but also impart valuable lessons to their children, shaping how the next generation perceives money, wealth, and fulfillment. Business owners and estate planners also have the chance to leave a legacy that mirrors their beliefs, providing a sustainable impact for years to come.

The journey of aligning your values with your financial goals is not a one-time activity but an ongoing commitment. It involves self-reflection, strategy, and a willingness to adapt. As you proceed through this book, you will uncover frameworks and strategies designed to harness the power of aligning values with financial goals. Embrace this process, keeping in mind that the true value of wealth lies not just in numbers, but in its ability to fulfill the life you envision.

Chapter 1:
Understanding Sustainable Investing

Sustainable investing is more than a trend; it's a methodology that aligns your financial goals with your values, promoting a future where profitability and positive impact coexist. At its core, this approach integrates environmental, social, and governance (ESG) factors into investment decisions, guiding a path toward ethical impact while still aiming for strong financial returns. By understanding how sustainable investing has evolved, we see a foundation in ethical investment strategies that have matured from exclusionary methods to inclusive and proactive strategies that seek long-term value creation. Grasping this transformation empowers investors—from individual novices to seasoned financial planners—to not only participate in but also drive societal and environmental change. This chapter illuminates the journey of sustainable investing, providing a compass as you navigate its complexities and uncover the potential to harmonize your aspirations for income with a meaningful contribution to our world.

The Evolution of Ethical Investment Strategies traces a fascinating path from niche to mainstream, reflecting society's broader changes and values. Sustainable investing arguably started as a ripple— a small wave of conscientious capital mainly focused on moral and ethical grounds. Early ethical investors in the 1960s and 70s were largely driven by social movements; they chose to avoid industries such as tobacco, alcohol, and firearms. This practice, known as negative screening, was the cornerstone of ethical investment strategies back then, emphasizing what to exclude from portfolios rather than what to include.

Over time, the ethical investing landscape evolved, mainly due to shifting societal norms and increased awareness of global challenges. Investors began to realize that they could exert influence not just by avoiding what they found objectionable, but by actively supporting businesses that aligned with their broader values. This transition marked the dawn of a more proactive approach, where 'sustainable investing' became a more fitting term as it spoke to the long-term impact on both society and the planet.

The adaptation to more comprehensive ethical investment strategies didn't happen overnight. It was a gradual shift influenced by pivotal moments in history. The environmental disasters of the late 20th century and early 21st century, such as oil spills and industrial pollution, highlighted the destructive potential of ignoring environmental responsibilities. Social issues, too, came to the fore with increasing demands for diversity, fair labor practices, and human rights considerations. Investors sought not just to do no harm but to actively contribute to positive societal changes.

The development of Environmental, Social, and Governance (ESG) criteria marked a significant turning point in ethical investing, moving beyond simple exclusionary practices. ESG offered a framework for assessing and integrating various aspects of responsible business practices into investment decision-making. They provided a way to compare companies not only on financial metrics but also on how effectively they managed environmental risks, their social impact, and their governance structures.

ESG wasn't just about altruism; it was also about performance. Investors started to notice that companies with strong ESG practices often managed risks better and had a better reputation, leading to improved long-term financial performance. In this light, ESG shifted from a niche interest to a mainstream strategy as investors recognized its potential for generating competitive financial returns alongside societal benefits. With this evolution, the investment community began to see the possibility of achieving both profit and purpose—a powerful combination that has driven the uptake of sustainable investment strategies.

As ethical investment strategies have matured, so too have the tools available to investors. Technology has played a crucial role in this evolution, allowing better data collection and analysis of ESG factors. With these tools, investors can make more informed decisions, tailoring their portfolios not only to ethical preferences but also to financial goals. The proliferation of ESG-focused funds and indices has further democratized access to sustainable investing, allowing even novice investors to participate in strategies aligned with their values.

In this ever-evolving landscape, ethical investment strategies have become highly customizable, allowing individual investors to define what 'ethical' means for them. Personalized portfolios can now reflect a wide range of values, from environmental preservation to social justice, enabling investors to be not just spectators in the global market, but active participants in shaping a better world.

Corporations are taking note, too. The shift in investor expectations has encouraged many businesses to improve their sustainability practices. Firms now understand that embracing ESG criteria isn't merely a compliance exercise, but a critical factor in attracting investment. This mutual influence between investors and businesses has created a feedback loop that reinforces sustainable practices across industries and markets.

However, implementing and evolving these strategies isn't without its challenges. Ethical investment strategies often require complex balancing acts to maintain both financial performance and adherence to values. Investors may face dilemmas about where to draw the line or how to prioritize competing interests within ESG criteria. Despite these challenges, the demand for ethical investment options continues to grow, spurred by increasing numbers of investors who are motivated by the desire to see their money drive positive change.

Looking forward, ethical investment strategies will likely continue to evolve as newer generations of investors, such as millennials and Gen Z, prioritize sustainability more than any cohort before. These investors are more likely to question traditional capitalism approaches and actively seek out investment opportunities that align with their personal beliefs. As technology continues to advance, providing greater transparency and accountability, ethical investment strategies will become even more integral to mainstream financial markets.

In conclusion, the evolution of ethical investment strategies reflects a dynamic intersection of societal values, technological advancements, and financial innovations. What began as isolated acts of conscientious objection has matured into a comprehensive approach to investing that balances financial returns with social and environmental responsibility. By understanding this evolution, we can appreciate how far we've come and anticipate where we might go, with each investment helping to shape a more sustainable and equitable future.

Assessing Environmental, Social, and Governance (ESG) Criteria is a crucial step for anyone looking to delve into sustainable investing. As we navigate this section, let's consider the impact that integrating ESG factors can have on shaping sustainable investment portfolios. ESG factors are non-financial performance indicators that examine how a company's operations affect the world around it. While this may sound straightforward, ESG analysis requires thoughtful consideration and a nuanced understanding of the criteria. By assessing these factors, investors can align their portfolios with their values, pursuing not just profit but also positive societal impact.

The idea of evaluating a company based merely on its financial performance is evolving. Today, many investors consider how a company manages its environmental impact. This shift is partly due to the growing awareness of climate change and its far-reaching implications. Under the environmental criteria, investors assess a company's carbon footprint, energy efficiency, waste management, and resource conservation efforts. Organizations that prioritize sustainability often outperform their peers in the long run, reinforcing the connection between sustainable practices and financial success. By focusing on environmental metrics, investors can direct their capital towards companies committed to reducing negative environmental impacts while supporting innovation in clean technology.

Social criteria encompass a company's relationships with its employees, suppliers, customers, and the communities where it operates. This might involve evaluating how a company upholds labor rights, engages with its local community, and manages its supply chain. Companies that demonstrate strong social responsibility frequently enjoy better employee morale, increased customer loyalty, and, consequently, enhanced financial performance. Investors interested in social metrics look for organizations that prioritize diversity and inclusion, commit to fair trade practices, and actively participate in positive community engagement. Such factors not only reflect a company's ethical standing but can also offer insights into its operational resilience and long-term viability.

Governance is the third pillar of the ESG framework, focusing on the internal systems and practices that govern a company. This includes board diversity, executive compensation, transparency, and shareholder rights. Effective governance can protect investors from various risks, from financial misconduct to reputational damage. Sound governance practices ensure that a company adheres to ethical guidelines and regulatory requirements, fostering trust in the market.

Assessors consider the balance of power within the company's board, the alignment of executive pay with performance, and the company's overall transparency in reporting. These governance insights help investors mitigate risks associated with corporate scandals or mismanagement, ultimately safeguarding their investments.

Evaluating ESG criteria involves both qualitative and quantitative analysis. To truly understand a company's ESG performance, investors must go beyond merely checking boxes. This means reviewing comprehensive reports, conducting stakeholder interviews, and considering third-party ESG ratings and indices. Such evaluations help investors make informed decisions that align with their values and financial goals. Additionally, ESG ratings can facilitate portfolio diversification, guiding investors away from potentially risky investments towards those with robust ethical practices.

The intricacies of assessing ESG criteria lie in the availability and transparency of relevant data. Despite advances in reporting standards and frameworks, investors often face challenges due to inconsistencies in data quality. To navigate these hurdles, leveraging tools like ESG data platforms and engaging with ESG specialists can enhance the accuracy of assessments. Collaboration between investors, companies, and standardized reporting bodies can further improve the reliability and comparability of ESG data, driving meaningful progress in sustainable investment practices.

A critical aspect of ESG investing is understanding how to weigh the various criteria according to personal investment goals. Not all investors prioritize the same elements; some may focus heavily on social aspects, while others prioritize environmental or governance issues. To construct a balanced and effective ESG-oriented portfolio, investors should identify which elements matter most to them and apply these preferences systematically. Institutions can often assist in this process by offering bespoke solutions and investment products tailored to specific ESG criteria focus areas, providing flexibility to match personal investment preferences.

Ultimately, the assessment of ESG criteria is about more than just ethical responsibility; it's about long-term resilience and adaptability. Companies that integrate ESG into their core strategies are better positioned to navigate future challenges and seize emerging opportunities. By considering ESG factors alongside traditional financial metrics, investors enhance their ability to achieve sustained growth, underpinned by a commitment to societal good. This integrated approach allows for a more comprehensive understanding of potential risks and opportunities, paving the way for a sustainable and profitable investment journey.

In conclusion, assessing Environmental, Social, and Governance criteria is a dynamic and essential process for any conscious investor. By prioritizing ESG considerations, investors can align their financial ambitions with their desire for positive impact. This alignment is not merely aspirational but reflects a pragmatic approach to managing both financial risk and societal change. Through diligent analysis and action, we can help foster a more sustainable world, ensuring long-term benefits for both ourselves and future generations.

Chapter 2:
Setting Your Investment Objectives

As we transition into "Setting Your Investment Objectives," it's essential to remember that your investment path should be as unique as your aspirations. Identifying your financial objectives isn't simply about growing wealth; it's about aligning your resources with what you truly value, whether that's building a legacy, supporting causes you care about, or ensuring a comfortable retirement. Start by defining both your financial and impact goals clearly. Then, consider how much risk you're willing to take and the time horizon you have for your investments. Remember, the role of philanthropy can also be crucial in crafting a portfolio that reflects your ethical standards and social values. Along this journey, stay motivated and inspired to tweak your objectives as your life dynamics shift. This chapter will guide you in forging a path that meets your needs and stays true to your principles, setting a solid foundation for all your investment decisions ahead.

Defining Your Financial and Impact Goals is an essential step in aligning your investment strategies with your personal values and aspirations. It forms the foundation of your investment journey by articulating what you wish to achieve not just financially, but also in terms of the societal and environmental impact you desire to support. This approach marries the traditional goal-setting process with a broader perspective, recognizing that our financial decisions do not exist in a vacuum but are intertwined with the world around us.

To start this process, begin by reflecting on your core values—what truly matters most to you. This could range from supporting clean energy initiatives, advocating for gender equality, or promoting local community development. Understanding these values will help you identify the types of investments that resonate with your beliefs. Consider writing these down as they will guide you in specifying detailed goals that encompass both financial returns and social impact.

Next, consider your financial objectives. Are you looking to build wealth over a long period, or are you raising funds for a short-term need such as a child's education or a home purchase? Determine whether your primary focus is income generation, capital appreciation, or a combination of both. Include time-bound targets to provide a clear road map for evaluating progress. While financial growth is important, balance this against your desire to create a positive impact on society and the environment.

Assessing your impact goals can be a bit more intricate as it requires you to quantify qualitative ideals. Develop specific, measurable objectives to monitor the results of your investments' impact. This might mean choosing to invest in companies with strong ESG (Environmental, Social, and Governance) ratings or selecting projects that report on clear social outcomes. Remember, the impact does not necessarily equate to immediate benefits—consider long-term implications and potential for systemic change.

Another critical aspect is to strike a balance between financial and impact goals. Sometimes, ethical investments can come with compromises on returns compared to traditional investments. However, there are strategies to mitigate this risk, including diversifying your portfolio or setting aside a portion specifically for high-impact, potentially lower-return opportunities.

As you lay out your investment objectives, remember to revisit and revise them periodically. The world is constantly evolving, and so are the mechanisms and opportunities for sustainable investing. Regularly assessing your goals ensures that they remain aligned with your values and the current global context.

Engage with a financial advisor well-versed in sustainable investing to further refine your goals. A knowledgeable advisor can provide insights into the developing landscape of impact measurement and guide you through the intricacies of aligning financial returns with ethical considerations. Collaboration with such professionals can ease the complexity and enhance the effectiveness of your investment strategy.

Moreover, mapping out your investment objectives becomes a motivating process rather than a checklist task. It empowers you to channel your ambitions into tangible outcomes, reinforcing the notion that investments can indeed be a force for good. Let your goals be a reflection of who you are and what you stand for, both financially and morally.

The exhilaration of seeing not just your financial portfolio grow, but also knowing that your money is contributing to sustainable progress, is unparalleled. Engage actively with your investments; stay informed and adjust as necessary to maximize impact. Realigning as necessary will turn your goals into stepping stones towards a sustainable legacy.

In summary, defining your financial and impact goals is not just procedural—it's transformational. It invites you into a higher purpose, where financial prowess and ethical integrity coexist harmoniously. Craft clear, actionable objectives and remain steadfast in your commitment to both fiscal health and positive societal contributions. This synergy will ultimately contribute to a more equitable and sustainable future.

Personal Risk Tolerance and Time Horizon are crucial elements of setting your investment objectives. These concepts may seem straightforward but they require deep introspection and understanding of one's financial and emotional capacity when it comes to market fluctuations. They're not just about numbers and percentages; they're fundamentally about how comfortably you can ride the ups and downs of investing. Balancing risk tolerance with investment goals requires a nuanced approach, where aligning financial targets with personal comfort levels ensures both peace of mind and a structured path toward those targets.

Simply put, personal risk tolerance is your ability to handle the unexpected twists in the investment journey. It embodies the level of unpredictability and potential loss you're willing—and can afford—to accept. On the other hand, your time horizon is the period over which you'll let your investments mature. Are you saving for a short-term goal like a vacation in a couple years, or are you eyeing a long-term objective such as retirement? Understanding the interplay between these aspects sets a foundation for making sound investment decisions.

Risk tolerance isn't static; it evolves with changes in personal circumstances. Consider a young professional just starting out. Their primary financial obligations might be minimal, allowing for a higher tolerance for risk with potential for greater returns. Conversely, a family with children approaching college age might prioritize preserving wealth over chasing high returns, thereby exhibiting a lower risk threshold. Understanding these shifts is essential for investors and advisors alike.

Time horizon also plays a critical role in shaping your investment strategies. Longer investment timelines generally allow for a higher risk tolerance, as there's ample time to recover from potential downturns. This can create opportunities to invest in assets with potentially higher volatility, like stocks, which traditionally offer higher returns over extended periods. Those with shorter horizons may prefer more stable investments, like bonds, where principal preservation is key.

Defining your personal risk tolerance is not only about financial capacity but emotional resilience too. It's one thing to plan on paper for a market downturn; it's another to emotionally weather the storm when it strikes. Some investors might lose sleep over a 10% drop in the market, while others see it as a buying opportunity. Indifference or panic during market fluctuations signals a misalignment with your true risk profile.

Financial planners often employ risk assessments or questionnaires to gauge risk tolerance. These tools measure your reaction to hypothetical financial scenarios and your investment knowledge, providing a baseline for subsequent investment decisions. However, beyond quizzes and surveys, understanding risk tolerance involves contemplating your fiscal safety nets, emotional responses to past financial decisions, and long-term aspirations.

Envision your planned milestones and the time frame for reaching them. Short, medium, and long-term goals each demand a tailored approach. Are you planning to buy a home in five years, or is early retirement part of your vision? For short-term goals, preserving capital might take precedence, while for longer-term objectives, the focus might lean towards aggressive growth.

History shows that markets are unpredictable. They swing, and sometimes dramatically. Your ability to withstand these swings and stay invested throughout is pivotal in achieving financial goals. It's crucial to known when to hold on and when adjustments could align better with evolving financial aspirations or life changes.

Moreover, as investors grow older or circumstances change (such as an inheritance or job change), risk tolerance and time horizons can adjust. This adaptability calls for periodic reviews and flexibility in evolving one's investment portfolio. Tailoring investment objectives ensures that they remain relevant and aligned with both current life phase and future aspirations.

Ultimately, aligning personal risk tolerance and time horizon with your investment strategy provides an informed pathway to your financial objectives. It brings purpose to your investment decisions, combining endurance and strategy in a volatile market environment. As you define these parameters, remember that success lies not just in understanding these concepts but also in harmoniously integrating them with your personal goals.

The Role of Philanthropy in Your Portfolio seamlessly blends with crafting investment objectives by aligning your financial strategies with personal values and social impact. As you delve into setting your investment objectives, consider philanthropy not just as an afterthought but as a core element. It's about envisioning philanthropy as more than just charitable giving; it's an integrative tool that can foster personal satisfaction while enhancing your portfolio's societal impact.

Incorporating philanthropy into your investment objectives requires a thorough understanding of how your values translate into actionable investment strategies. Begin by identifying causes you truly care about. Is it environmental sustainability, educational programs, healthcare improvements, or something personal? Reflecting on your passions allows you to craft a financial plan that reflects the profound intersection between personal value and broader societal good.

Your financial and impact goals serve as the foundational guideposts when pairing philanthropy with investment. By caring for the environment through ESG (Environmental, Social, and Governance) investments, you put money into funds that echo sustainability, simultaneously nurturing potential returns. Socially responsible investing doesn't negate profitability but emphasizes purpose, expanding traditional views of financial success to encompass social progress.

Setting clear, personalized goals helps to illuminate the path forward. For some, that may involve establishing a family foundation, offering a substantial vehicle to direct your philanthropic vision with a long-term impact that echoes your core values. Philanthropy, in this context, functions as a strategic component of sustainable wealth management, supporting causes and communities over generations.

Moreover, when incorporating philanthropy into your portfolio, risk tolerance must not be sidelined. This is an area where thoughtful deliberation on time horizons plays a pivotal role. Are you in a position to take immediate high-impact actions, or is a gradual, methodical philanthropic investment more suitable? Balancing immediate desires with long-term commitments is crucial to ensuring a stable yet flexible portfolio strategy.

Integrating philanthropy with investment objectives goes beyond financial contributions. It's about making investments that embody the values you'd like to promote and support. Participation in shareholder advocacy, for instance, allows you to influence corporate policies for greater ethical practices. Interlinking investment stewardship with intentional giving creates a distinctive blend where financial growth meets purposeful change.

Your philanthropic strategy can also be a motivating factor in motivating family and community engagement. It's a unique opportunity to educate future generations on both the importance of financial literacy and the power of giving back. Encouraging family discussions about wealth and generosity fosters a legacy that's as much about monetary success as it is about sustained social responsibility.

A holistic portfolio considers not just what you own but what you give. Philanthropy reinforces the social fabric that binds ethical investment together, nurturing both financial ecosystems and communities. Through planned giving, direct donations, or impact-focused investments, your portfolio can act as a catalyst for innovation and change, driving progress in sectors you'd like to see thrive.

Incorporate regular evaluations to ensure your philanthropic focuses align with evolving personal and societal needs. Revisiting your strategies periodically and being open to adjustments can lead to more impactful giving. Changes in life circumstances, regulatory environments, or even shifts in societal challenges can prompt necessary recalibrations to ensure your philanthropic direction remains relevant and effective.

The role of philanthropy in your portfolio isn't just a strategy; for many, it represents the profound joy that comes with making a tangible difference. Through detailed planning and intentional action, it becomes a statement of your commitment to a better world. Your financial plans are an extension of your identity, and integrating philanthropy moves you from being a participant to a leader in the quest for societal progress.

Chapter 3:
Crafting a Sustainable
Investment Policy Statement

Crafting a sustainable investment policy statement is your compass for navigating the evolving landscape of sustainable investing. It merges your financial goals with your ethical values, serving as a dynamic blueprint for decision-making. Start by defining your personal investment beliefs and understand the nuances of integrating Environmental, Social, and Governance (ESG) factors into your strategy without missing the opportunity to reflect your unique constraints and aspirations. This statement isn't static; it evolves as markets shift and your values deepen, so regularly monitor and revise it to ensure it remains aligned with both current realities and future aspirations. By committing to a thoughtful and flexible policy, you empower yourself to pursue financial growth while making a positive impact, ultimately bringing your investment philosophy to life in a way that resonates with the world you wish to influence.

Establishing Your Investment Beliefs and Restrictions involves embarking on a journey of self-discovery and introspection to assess how your values align with your financial endeavors. At its core, this process is about understanding what's truly important to you and using that information to shape an investment portfolio that reflects your personal ethos. Whether you're an individual investor, a family planning for the future, or an asset manager looking to balance clients' interests, recognizing these beliefs is the cornerstone of crafting a resilient, meaningful investment policy statement.

First, let's explore what investment beliefs are and why they matter. Think of them as the principles or guidelines that will govern how you make investment decisions. These beliefs could stem from a range of factors: personal values, worldview, past experiences, or even aspirations for positive societal impact. For example, an individual deeply concerned about climate change might prioritize investments in companies actively working to reduce carbon emissions. Conversely, a business owner with a keen eye on governance might favor firms with robust ethical standards and transparency in operations.

Your personal investment beliefs can significantly influence the structure of your portfolio. They can direct you toward certain sectors, industries, or asset classes that resonate with your values. But it's not just about what you invest in; it's also about how you invest. Are you inclined towards passive index funds that offer broad exposure with low costs, or are you drawn to actively managed portfolios where managers seek to achieve specific socio-environmental outcomes? Do these philosophical outlooks on investment coincide with your willingness to take risks or the time horizon over which you plan to invest?

It's crucial to note that defining these beliefs isn't a static process. Your views may evolve as you grow, learn, and experience new things. Economic conditions change, new technologies disrupt markets, and unforeseen global events can shift your perspective. The key is to remain flexible, allowing your investment philosophy to adapt over time while staying grounded in core principles. This adaptability ensures that your investment strategy remains relevant, authentic, and aligned with your overarching goals.

Now, let's turn our attention to restrictions—what you consciously choose to exclude from your investment portfolio. These can be based on personal ethics, legal considerations, or financial prudence. Some investors might decide to avoid industries that conflict with their moral standpoint, like tobacco or weapons manufacturing. Others may set financial restrictions, such as avoiding investments that exceed a certain risk threshold or maintaining a specific liquidity level for personal or business needs.

Establishing such restrictions helps you create and maintain a disciplined approach to investing. It minimizes the emotional or impulsive decisions that can lead to poor financial outcomes and keeps the focus on long-term objectives. Restrictions serve not only as protective barriers but also as a clarifying filter through which potential investment opportunities are evaluated.

Consider the role of ESG (Environmental, Social, and Governance) factors as a bridge between your beliefs and restrictions. ESG criteria provide a framework to assess investments against your values. By integrating these factors into your policy statement, you formalize your commitment to sustainability and social responsibility. ESG criteria can guide the selection of funds, inform due diligence processes, and ensure that your portfolio aligns with both your ethical standards and financial objectives.

A vital step is documenting these beliefs and restrictions clearly in your investment policy statement. This documentation serves multiple purposes. It's a reference tool that keeps your strategy anchored during market fluctuations, a communication piece for advisors and family members, and a historical record that can be reviewed and revised periodically to ensure it stays relevant.

Effective communication with financial professionals is another benefit of clearly established beliefs and restrictions. When advisors understand your ethos and boundaries, they can provide more targeted recommendations and better strategies to align with your vision. They can help you navigate complex financial landscapes with a clear understanding of what you value and aim to avoid.

Moreover, by establishing and articulating your investment beliefs and restrictions, you lay the groundwork for greater personal and financial fulfillment. You're not just chasing returns; you're making decisions that contribute to a broader purpose. This alignment enriches your investment journey, fostering satisfaction that extends beyond financial gains, contributing positively to the world you wish to support.

In conclusion, our investment beliefs and restrictions play a monumental role in crafting a sustainable investment policy that is as unique as the individuals and entities it represents. Embrace this exploratory process. Engage with it deeply and intentionally, realizing that this foundational work is essential for aligning wealth with purpose. As you continue on this path, remember that the goal isn't merely wealth accumulation, but building a legacy with impact and intention, truly making a difference with each investment choice.

Integrating ESG Factors into Investment Policy is more than a buzzword; it's a crucial aspect of sustainable investing that personalizes your portfolio to align with your ethical and financial objectives. As we navigate the shift from traditional investing towards a more sustainable approach, integrating Environmental, Social, and Governance (ESG) factors becomes a vital part of crafting your investment policy statement. But how do you effectively incorporate these elements to not only enhance your portfolio's potential but also remain true to your values? Let's delve into the strategies and considerations that can guide this integration.

ESG integration begins with a deep understanding of what these factors represent. Environmental considerations might include a company's carbon footprint, waste management practices, and energy efficiency measures. Social factors can examine a company's labor practices, community engagement, and human rights record, while governance might focus on corporate policies, executive compensation, and board diversity. Together, these elements provide a holistic view of a company's operations, risks, and long-term sustainability.

Translating these factors into your investment policy requires a clear definition of your values, priorities, and expectations. Essentially, your investment policy statement should articulate your commitment to sustainability alongside traditional financial goals. This sets a foundation for making informed decisions going forward, influencing how you select assets, engage with companies, and monitor performance.

Start by assessing your current values and how they align with available ESG criteria. Are you more concerned with environmental impact or social governance? Such introspection will help you prioritize issues that matter most, helping you filter the vast array of ESG data available. You might choose to invest in companies with strong environmental policies but must also evaluate how these practices affect financial performance. One effective approach is to establish ESG-specific guidelines within your policy, helping you to clearly assess potential investments.

Formulating these guidelines might seem daunting, but it doesn't need to be overly complex. Begin with simple rules that reflect your highest priorities. For instance, you could decide to avoid investments in industries with significant environmental harm, like fossil fuels, or in companies failing to demonstrate adequate labor rights protections. These baseline exclusions can significantly focus your investment universe.

However, exclusions aren't the only route. There's potential for positive reinforcement by seeking out firms actively contributing to social welfare or environmental sustainability. This proactive approach not only aligns with your values but often identifies opportunities in burgeoning sectors like renewable energy or sustainable agriculture. By identifying leading ESG performers, you fulfill your ethical mandates while potentially securing promising financial returns.

The next step is integrating these criteria with the traditional financial analysis you'd ordinarily perform. ESG factors serve as complementary data, enhancing your understanding of a company's long-term prospects and sustainability posture. For investors and advisors, this dual assessment ensures decisions consider both current performance metrics and longer-term sustainability risks and opportunities.

It's crucial to recognize that sustainable investing isn't about sacrificing gains; it's about enduring value. ESG factors may help reveal non-financial risks that traditional analyses overlook. For instance, a company with poor environmental records may face future regulations leading to high fines or operational costs. Conversely, firms with robust governance structures typically exhibit resilience during economic downturns, preserving shareholder value in the long run.

Working ESG considerations into your investment policy also requires monitoring and revising these guidelines as the field evolves. ESG standards and reporting are still developing, and as such, staying adaptable and informed is essential. Regularly reviewing both your policy and your portfolio ensures they remain synchronized with your values and latest industry standards. Once set, your policy shouldn't be static; it should evolve with your wealth strategy and societal progress.

For those new to ESG investing, engaging with a financial advisor knowledgeable in sustainable investments could be invaluable. These professionals can assist in crafting precise policy statements, ensuring consistent application of your ESG criteria across the investment process. In today's market, robo-advisors and digital platforms also offer ESG customizations, providing convenient options for maintaining and monitoring investment adherence to set guidelines.

In conclusion, integrating ESG factors into your investment policy isn't just socially responsible; it's financially savvy. This alignment demands diligence, introspection, and continual adaptation. But as the global focus on sustainability accelerates, possessing a well-crafted policy addresses present concerns and secures long-term investment health. By embracing ESG, you're not just investing in companies; you're investing in a sustainable future and aligning your financial legacy with enduring social and environmental values.

Monitoring and Revising Your Investment Policy is a crucial step in crafting a sustainable investment policy statement that aligns with your evolving financial goals and values. As life progresses, both personal and market conditions inevitably change, making it necessary to routinely assess and adjust your investment policy. Maintaining flexibility in your strategy ensures that your investments not only remain aligned with current goals but also adapt to unforeseen circumstances.

A well-crafted investment policy statement (IPS) should serve as the foundation for ongoing evaluation. It's not a static document, but rather a living guide that requires regular updates. The primary purpose of monitoring your investment policy is to stay informed about whether the original assumptions and constraints still hold true. Are your financial and impact goals still relevant? Have there been any significant changes in your personal circumstances like career transitions, family needs, or lifestyle adjustments? Staying attentive to these factors will help ensure your IPS remains relevant and effective.

Investment markets themselves are in a constant state of flux. Economic cycles, technological advancements, and policy changes continuously create new opportunities and challenges. For example, shifts in regulations can influence which sustainable investments qualify as ESG-compliant. Staying vigilant in understanding the broader market environment means reassessing the criteria and benchmarks used to evaluate your performance. This doesn't mean reacting to every market news headline, but rather maintaining a strategic perspective.

Setting benchmarks doesn't just provide a means for comparison; it provides clarity on whether your strategy is working. However, just as the landscape evolves, so too should your benchmarks. If the benchmark doesn't accurately capture what you aim to achieve through your investment policy, it may render your assessments ineffective. Therefore, part of the process in revising your IPS includes reevaluating whether the metrics for success align with your current objectives and the broader market climate.

Effective monitoring should incorporate both qualitative and quantitative reviews. Quantitative assessments involve closely examining investment performance, fees, and returns in the context of your predefined benchmarks. Meanwhile, qualitative reviews consider the alignment of your investments with personal values and sustainability goals. Both aspects are essential, as financial returns and value-based impacts often go hand-in-hand in sustainable investing.

Communicating with financial advisors or planners is another vital part of the monitoring process. Given their expertise, advisors can provide invaluable insight into market trends, risk management strategies, and potential opportunities you may not be fully aware of. They play a crucial role in bringing external viewpoints into your internal decision-making process, offering a broader perspective that can be beneficial in the frequent reconsideration of your IPS.

Risk assessment is also crucial when revising your IPS. Life events, such as marriage, purchasing a home, or preparing for children's education, will modify your risk profile. Regularly updating the IPS ensures that the chosen investment tactics reflect these life stages, accommodating both short-term liquidity needs and long-term sustainability goals.

Align your ongoing IPS review with routine life audits, a time when you assess broader financial health, including income, expenses, debts, and savings. Synchronizing these reviews makes it easier to see the broader picture and determine whether your investment strategies need recalibrating based on changes in financial circumstances, personal priorities, or markets.

Moreover, integrating new ESG developments into your policy is necessary to maintain its relevance. ESG criteria are not set in stone; they are continuously evolving. Innovations like new clean technologies or changes in company practices may shift your preference in certain industries or companies. Regular monitoring allows you to identify these trends early and adjust your holdings accordingly to ensure they remain in line with both financial aspirations and personal ethics.

Reflecting on your initial motivations for sustainable investing provides direction for revisits and revisions. Are the portfolio strategies effectively accomplishing what they set out to do? This includes both financial returns and impact goals, which should coalesce to create not just wealth, but a meaningful contribution to social or environmental initiatives. As you progress in your sustainable investing journey, having clarity on these motivations will guide revisions and eventual policy refinement.

Finally, commit to a periodic review schedule. This could be annually, semi-annually, or even quarterly, depending on comfort level and how rapid your life or markets change. The key is consistency in reviewing, with an open mind to adapt your policies and strategies. By doing so, your investment policy statement becomes a dynamic tool that drives both financial success and personal fulfillment, navigating the inevitable changes life presents.

Chapter 4:
Asset Allocation for the Conscious Investor

Deciding where to put your money can feel like piecing together a complex puzzle, but for the conscious investor, it's about creating harmony between financial success and ethical integrity. Asset allocation is more than just spreading investments across different asset classes; it's a dynamic strategy that respects your values. A conscious investor understands that choosing how to diversify isn't merely about maximizing returns; it's about crafting a portfolio that positively impacts the world. With the unique demands of sustainability, your approach will likely differ from traditional models, requiring innovative thinking to integrate social and environmental considerations. While balancing sustainable bonds, equities, and other green assets, focus on purpose-driven diversification that aligns with your long-term vision and values. This isn't just about personal gain; it's about fostering a future where financial health and moral responsibility go hand in hand. In doing so, you're not just building wealth but consciously contributing to a more sustainable world for yourself and future generations.

Strategies for Diversification in Sustainable Investing within the chapter "Asset Allocation for the Conscious Investor" emphasizes the importance of balancing financial return with environmental, social, and governance (ESG) impact. The concept of diversification is vital in sustainable investing, aiming not only to minimize risk but also to maximize positive impact on society and the environment. For the conscious investor, diversification takes on a new layer of complexity as it involves aligning a portfolio with personal values while maintaining financial performance.

To effectively diversify in sustainable investing, one must begin with a clear understanding of which asset classes align with their values. Stocks, bonds, mutual funds, and alternative investments each offer unique opportunities for positive ESG impact. An investor may target industries that prioritize clean energy, develop social initiatives, or demonstrate sound governance practices. While the conventional wisdom of diversification advises spreading investments across sectors and geographies, a conscientious approach involves selecting assets that are also diverse in their ESG impact ratings.

Investors can look at thematic investments as a strategic approach to diversification. This involves focusing on themes like renewable energy, sustainable agriculture, or technology aimed at solving environmental issues. Each theme can add a layer of security to a portfolio by meeting global demands and leveraging innovations. For example, investing in renewable energy companies not only lies in a high-growth sector but also mitigates exposure to the risks related to fossil fuels, which are subject to regulatory changes and societal pressure.

Moreover, impact investing, a growing niche within sustainable finance, offers another avenue for diversification. By targeting investments that intend to generate positive and measurable social and environmental impacts alongside financial returns, individuals can align portfolios more closely with values. Impact investments can span various asset classes and sectors, from green bonds to community-focused funds. The key is to assess and balance the potential for both financial returns and ESG outcomes.

A diversified portfolio for a conscious investor also involves mixed maturity profiles and risk levels within chosen sustainable investments.

Longer-term holdings such as green infrastructure projects or forestry investments can pair well with shorter-term, liquid ESG-friendly stocks or bonds. This mixed timeline strategy ensures ongoing cash flow while supporting larger projects that yield substantial environmental benefits over the long run.

Maintaining a robust level of diversification requires continuous monitoring and proactive management. The sustainable investment space evolves rapidly, with new regulations, technologies, and consumer sentiments continually reshaping the landscape. Investors should periodically assess the ESG performance and impact of their portfolios, adjusting allocations to reflect updates in their personal values or in the ESG profile of their investments. Regular rebalancing based on financial performance and ethical considerations strengthens the alignment of portfolios with both financial goals and sustainability objectives.

Incorporating real estate and alternative investments can further enhance diversification endeavors. Green real estate, for example, provides ongoing income streams through rental payments while contributing to building sustainable cities. Similarly, investing in certified sustainable timberland not only counters deforestation but also serves as a countercyclical asset in an economic downturn.

It's important to note that diversification goes beyond merely selecting different asset classes; it extends to incorporating various investment styles. An investor might choose a passive investment approach through ESG index funds or opt for active management via ESG-focused hedge funds. Each method has its advantages, and conscientious investors may use a combination to benefit from both stability and targeted impact.

The role of technology in diversification strategies can't be overlooked. Leveraging big data analytics, AI, and blockchain can aid in capturing, analyzing, and managing ESG data more effectively, providing deeper insights into potential investments. These technological solutions ensure that asset allocation aligns with the dynamic nature of ESG factors, facilitating informed decision-making.

While it might seem daunting, sustainable investing doesn't mean sacrificing returns for ethical considerations. Instead, with a comprehensive diversification strategy, it's possible to create a balanced portfolio that respects personal values and pursuit of wealth growth. As investors navigate through asset allocation for conscious investing, they forge a path to not only a prosperous financial future, but also a sustainable world for generations to come.

Asset Classes in a Sustainable Portfolio represent the unique blend required to create a diversified yet values-driven investment approach for today's conscious investors. Constructing a sustainable portfolio isn't merely about avoiding harm; it's about actively choosing investments that contribute positively to society and the environment. This involves including a variety of asset classes that align with Environmental, Social, and Governance (ESG) principles, alongside financial goals. By integrating sustainability into each asset class, investors can aim for growth while ensuring their money supports constructive outcomes.

Equities, or stocks, are often at the core of any portfolio, and for those focused on sustainability, they offer a platform to drive change. Sustainable equities focus on companies that meet ESG criteria, meaning they are involved in activities that promote environmental stewardship, social responsibility, and sound governance practices. One can consider investing in companies pursuing renewable energy technologies, improving labor practices, or those that have transparency in their corporate governance. The advantage of investing in sustainable stocks lies not just in potential returns, but also in shareholder power to influence corporate policies towards sustainability.

Fixed Income securities, including bonds, provide stability to a portfolio. Within a sustainable framework, green and social bonds have become prominent. These instruments allow governments and corporations to raise money specifically for projects tackling climate change or addressing social issues, such as affordable housing or education. Investors in these bonds can take solace in the knowledge that their investments are directly funding initiatives that aim to drive tangible positive changes in the world. Over recent years, the market for green bonds has grown substantially, offering ample opportunities for investors looking to balance risk-return with societal impact.

For the diversified investor, alternative assets play a critical role. These may include investments like real estate, commodities, or private equity, each of which can be aligned with sustainability goals. Real estate investment trusts (REITs), focusing on environmentally friendly buildings, such as those with green certifications, have attracted significant interest due to their dual benefit of income and capital appreciation potential. Similarly, commodities tied to sustainable practices, like responsibly sourced timber or metals critical for sustainable technologies, offer unique portfolio diversification benefits while adhering to ethical standards.

Investment in sustainable infrastructure is gaining prominence as it presents pathways to develop essential services and resources in a manner that minimizes environmental footprint. Examples include renewable energy projects, water treatment facilities, and public transportation developments. These projects not only fulfill a pressing demand for infrastructure but also promise steady cash flows and resilient long-term returns. Engaging in such infrastructure ventures can allow investors to hedge their portfolios against traditional market volatility through an asset class known for stability and utility-like growth trajectories.

Certainly, one cannot overlook the role of cash and cash equivalents in a sustainable portfolio. Although often relegated to stability or liquidity purposes, these funds can also align with sustainable principles. By placing cash in banks with strong green banking policies or community development financial institutions, investors support the flow of capital to projects that prioritize sustainability and impact under-served communities. Carefully choosing where to park liquid assets can subtly, yet influentially, support positive financial ecosystems.

Lastly, engaging with funds or exchange-traded funds (ETFs) that concentrate on ESG themes offers investors a compact and effective route to align with their sustainability aspirations. These funds provide instant diversification, spreading investment over numerous companies or bonds screened for ESG criteria. Actively or passively managed, ESG-themed funds can cater to varying risk appetites and investment priorities. They streamline the process of investing sustainably for those who lack the time or expertise to evaluate single securities individually.

Integrating these diverse asset classes forms the tapestry of a sustainable portfolio that not only aims to achieve financial targets but also contributes to societal welfare and environmental protection. Conscious investors must regularly revisit their asset mix, checking alignment with both personal values and market opportunities. As the landscape of sustainable investing evolves, so too must the portfolios, navigating new classes and instruments that promise growth while fostering a sustainable future. The journey of sustainable investing invites participation in a broader movement where the power of capital meets the purpose of change.

Rebalancing with Purpose offers a transformative approach to maintaining an investment strategy that reflects your personal values and financial aspirations. It's not merely about adjusting your portfolio to meet market conditions; it's about realigning your investments with your evolving goals and the principles that guide your life. For the conscious investor, rebalancing demands an extra layer of intention. It's an ongoing process that calls for thoughtfulness, discipline, and a deep understanding of how each asset contributes to both financial returns and societal impact.

You might be wondering how this aligns with the greater mission of sustainable investing. Well, the connection is profound and multifaceted. In essence, rebalancing with purpose ties together the broad threads of ethical commitment and financial savvy. It's about reviewing your portfolio regularly, assessing not only its market performance but also its alignment with environmental, social, and governance (ESG) criteria. Here, the goal isn't just profit maximization but striking a balance between returns and responsible investing.

Imagine you've invested in a variety of sectors, focusing on high-growth opportunities that align with your environmental beliefs. Suppose the market shifts, and suddenly, some sectors outperform others, skewing your portfolio's balance and diminishing its alignment with your values. Rebalancing becomes crucial. It ensures your portfolio stays dynamic and true to your intentions, making strategic adjustments rather than reactive decisions.

Rebalancing isn't merely about selling high and buying low, although that classic strategy plays a role. It's also a chance to reflect on new insights or shifts in personal values that might change how you weigh investments in certain industries. Perhaps you've become more aware of the social impact of a particular industry or have gained greater insight into renewable energies. These evolutions in understanding can affect how you perceive risk versus reward.

Rebalancing with purpose isn't a solo endeavor confined to algorithm-determined transactions. It involves setting specific, personal parameters that guide your strategies. For example, rather than simply targeting a 70/30 stock-to-bond ratio, a conscious investor would consider how each element within that ratio serves broader goals beyond the bottom line. Does the stock portion favor companies with robust sustainability policies? Are the bonds supporting green initiatives?

Let's delve into the process. Start by examining your current asset allocation. Compare it against your ideal portfolio—the one that balances financial objectives with sustainable and ethical considerations. Are there discrepancies? If so, take deliberate actions to address them. This might involve increasing exposure to high-impact sectors or divesting from assets that no longer align with your criteria.

Engagement with professionals can provide critical insights into effective rebalancing. Financial advisors specializing in ESG criteria offer expertise that can align your investment strategy with evolving personal values. Moreover, they can guide decisions on adjusting asset classes or exploring new investment vehicles more aligned with your goals.

Automated tools and platforms can also aid this process, providing dashboards and analytics that make it easier to recognize when your portfolio drifts from its target allocations. Some platforms even offer alerts for when rebalancing should occur, adding convenience to the conscientious investor's toolkit. However, apply these tools as aids, not replacements, for personal judgment and intention.

A periodic review schedule is fundamental. Quarterly or semi-annual reviews can help maintain vigilance, yet there is no one-size-fits-all. The cadence should reflect your investment strategy's complexity, the volatility of chosen industries, and personal risk tolerance. Importantly, every review should stay rooted in core values—resist the temptation to make hasty changes driven by short-term market fluctuations.

Consider the tax implications of rebalancing. Selling certain investments to realign your portfolio might trigger capital gains taxes, a factor that's important to weigh against the benefits of rebalancing. Utilizing tax-advantaged accounts or engaging in tax-loss harvesting strategies could mitigate some of these impacts, ensuring that your efforts to balance purpose and profit don't incur unnecessary costs.

Finally, rebalancing is a statement of intention. It affirms your dedication to a holistic investment philosophy that prioritizes both ethical objectives and financial imperatives. As you refine your portfolio to better reflect your aspirations and values, you exert greater influence over your financial destiny and the societal changes you wish to see.

The conscious investor treats rebalancing not as a chore, but as a pivotal exercise in testament to mindful stewardship. Each decision underscores a commitment to doing what you believe is right, for yourself and for the world. Remember, effective rebalancing is significantly more than numbers on a spreadsheet—it's an opportunity for continual growth, reflection, and reaffirmation of your dedication to a purposeful path in a rapidly evolving financial landscape.

Chapter 5:
Risk Management in Socially Responsible Investing

In the dynamic landscape of socially responsible investing (SRI), the act of managing risk isn't just about safeguarding assets—it's about aligning your investment strategy with your values while maintaining financial health. With ESG factors now sharply in focus, investors face unique challenges that differ from conventional investing experiences. Balancing ethical considerations with financial returns can be a delicate art, requiring an understanding of how these elements interact. Investors must consider how ESG-related risks like regulatory changes, climate impacts, and social movements could influence returns and volatility. Effective risk management tools, ranging from diversified portfolios to ESG-focused insurance products, can help mitigate potential drawbacks without compromising on values. By strategically assessing and integrating these components, investors can craft a robust portfolio that not only aims for financial growth but also contributes positively to societal goals, inspiring greater confidence and commitment in pursuing a sustainable investment journey.

Understanding the Risks Unique to ESG Investing as we dive into socially responsible investing, it's crucial to recognize that every investment strategy has its own particular set of risks. ESG investing, while aligned with ethical goals and focused on driving positive change, is no exception. The unique risks associated with ESG investments can impact their financial performance, volatility, and suitability for investors with differing risk tolerances. Understanding these risks isn't just about safeguarding returns, it's about ensuring that the investment strategy remains true to your values and long-term objectives.

One of the primary risks associated with ESG investing is the potential for variability in how ESG factors are assessed and weighted. Unlike traditional financial metrics, which are largely standardized and quantifiable, ESG criteria can be subjective and variable across industries and geographies. This lack of standardization can lead to discrepancies between ESG ratings from different providers, making it challenging for investors to accurately assess the ESG profile of a given investment. As a result, two funds claiming to be ESG-compliant might hold vastly different companies.

Then there's the issue of data availability and accuracy. Companies are under increasing pressure to disclose ESG-related information, but the level and quality of disclosure can vary greatly. This inconsistency not only complicates the evaluation process but can lead to potential informational asymmetries where certain investors may have access to better or more timely data than others. This can be particularly concerning when considering smaller companies or those in emerging markets, where ESG reporting practices may not be as robust or transparent.

Moreover, ESG investing often involves balancing financial returns with broader societal or environmental outcomes. This dual mandate can sometimes result in trade-offs between maximizing returns and adhering to ESG principles. For example, choosing to exclude certain sectors such as fossil fuels can limit diversification, potentially increasing the portfolio's volatility. Investors need to be clear about how much emphasis they want to place on financial returns versus ESG goals and what that means for their overall risk profile.

Geopolitical factors also play a significant role in ESG investing. As governments globally drive policy changes to address climate change and social equality, these shifts can create opportunities but also risks. Policy changes can impact the cost of business or alter the competitive landscape, and companies that are slow to adapt may face financial or reputational repercussions. In contrast, companies that are well-aligned with such policies may gain a competitive edge. Keeping a pulse on evolving regulations and geopolitical dynamics is critical for ESG investors.

There's also the emerging risk of "greenwashing," where companies or investment products claim to be more environmentally or socially responsible than they truly are. This misrepresentation can lead to reputational damage and financial losses for investors if they purchase assets based on incomplete or misleading information. Navigating the fine line between genuine ESG initiatives and marketing spin requires careful due diligence and a critical eye.

Another emerging risk is technology disruption. As the world moves towards a more sustainable future, technological innovations are likely to disrupt traditional business models and create new sectors. While this can present opportunities for ESG investors, it also brings uncertainties. Firms that are unable to adapt to technological changes may lose their market position, impacting ESG funds that have invested heavily in them.

Understanding the risks unique to ESG investing requires a proactive approach, one that includes staying informed about global trends, scrutinizing data quality, and critically assessing the alignment of ESG strategies with personal financial goals. Investors should consider partnering with knowledgeable advisors who can offer insights into these complex areas, helping them to make informed decisions that align with both their financial and ESG objectives.

In managing these risks, diversification remains a critical strategy. By spreading investments across different asset classes, regions, and sectors, investors can mitigate some of the volatility associated with ESG strategies. Additionally, regular monitoring and rebalancing of portfolios can help maintain alignment with changing ESG landscapes and personal investment objectives.

Ultimately, the goal of ESG investing is to harmonize financial performance with positive societal outcomes. By understanding the risks involved, investors can craft a strategy that not only aligns with their values but also positions them to navigate potential pitfalls. This balance ensures that investments remain resilient and relevant in a rapidly changing world.

Tools for Managing Investment Risk are essential for navigating the evolving landscape of socially responsible investing (SRI). As we delve deeper into this nuanced area, it's crucial to recognize that the integration of environmental, social, and governance (ESG) factors brings unique challenges and opportunities. Risk management tools must therefore be adept at addressing both traditional financial risks and those specific to ESG considerations.

One significant aspect of managing investment risk in SRI is the incorporation of ESG data analytics. By harnessing advanced data analytics, investors can gain deeper insights into potential risks and opportunities associated with ESG factors. This involves analyzing a wide array of data points, from carbon emissions and labor practices to corporate governance structures. Advanced analytics can highlight areas of concern before they materialize into financial issues, offering investors the chance to adjust their strategies proactively.

Moreover, investors can leverage qualitative and quantitative risk assessment frameworks to evaluate ESG risks. Qualitative assessments involve narrative evaluations of companies' ESG practices, which can be subjective but are valuable for understanding the broader context.

On the other hand, quantitative assessments rely on metrics and scores provided by ESG rating agencies. Combining these approaches offers a balanced view, allowing investors to tailor their strategies to align with their values while minimizing risk.

Stress testing and scenario analysis also play pivotal roles in managing investment risk within SRI. By simulating various economic, environmental, and social scenarios, investors can assess how their portfolios might perform under different conditions. This enables the identification of potential vulnerabilities and the development of strategies to bolster portfolio resilience. For instance, stress tests can reveal how a portfolio would fare in the face of regulatory changes related to climate policy, helping investors prepare for such transformations.

Effective diversification remains a cornerstone of risk management in any investment strategy, and it's no different for SRI. Diversifying not only across asset classes but also within ESG themes can distribute risk and enhance potential returns. For example, an investor might allocate funds across renewable energy projects, sustainable agriculture, and companies with strong governance scores. This thematic diversification helps buffer against sector-specific downturns while supporting a broader commitment to sustainability.

An often underappreciated tool is active engagement and shareholder advocacy. Through these approaches, investors can influence corporate behavior, prompting companies to adopt more sustainable and responsible practices. By actively engaging with companies, investors not only mitigate ESG risks but also drive positive change, aligning financial performance with ESG outcomes. Such activities range from dialogues with corporate leadership to submitting shareholder proposals, all aimed at effecting long-term, systemic change.

Additionally, insurance products designed for ESG risks are becoming increasingly prevalent. These products offer coverage for specific ESG-related incidents, such as environmental liabilities or social governance breaches. They provide an extra layer of security, helping protect investors' portfolios from potential losses stemming from unforeseen events related to ESG factors. As these insurance solutions continue to evolve, they offer valuable risk mitigation options for socially responsible investors.

Utilizing a robust investment policy statement (IPS) tailored to socially responsible investing is another foundational tool. An IPS outlines investment goals, risk tolerance, ESG criteria, and strategic asset allocations. It's a living document that guides investment decisions while providing a framework for responding to market and ESG-related changes. Regularly revisiting and revising the IPS ensures that it remains aligned with an investor's evolving values and goals.

Risk management in SRI also benefits from collaboration with financial advisors who specialize in ESG investing. These professionals bring expertise in identifying suitable investment opportunities, analyzing risks, and constructing portfolios that reflect investors' values. A knowledgeable advisor can navigate complex issues such as ESG data interpretation and thematic diversification, offering tailored guidance and support.

Furthermore, fostering continuous education around sustainable investing principles enhances risk management strategies. Investors committed to staying informed about evolving ESG criteria, regulatory developments, and emerging trends are better equipped to adapt their approaches. Workshops, webinars, and reading materials from credible sources contribute to a deeper understanding of how to manage risks effectively in the SRI landscape.

Investment technology has also advanced significantly, providing tools that automate and optimize risk management processes.

Platforms featuring AI and machine learning algorithms can analyze large datasets to predict potential ESG-related risks and opportunities, offering insights that might be overlooked through traditional analysis. These technological capabilities can streamline decision-making, ensuring that investors remain agile and informed.

Understanding the regulatory environment is another critical component. As governments increasingly introduce regulations relating to sustainability, investors must be aware of these shifts to adapt their strategies accordingly. A proactive approach includes engaging with policymakers and industry groups to stay ahead of regulatory changes that could impact ESG investment themes.

Lastly, fostering a long-term investment mindset is a psychological tool that helps manage both financial and ESG-related risks. By focusing on sustainable, long-term goals rather than short-term market fluctuations, investors can withstand volatility. This approach allows for a more consistent strategy that integrates ESG factors without being swayed by transient market trends.

In conclusion, the landscape of risk management within socially responsible investing is rich with tools and strategies that address both traditional and ESG-specific challenges. By employing a multifaceted approach—encompassing data analytics, diversification, stakeholder engagement, and continuous education—investors can align their portfolios with their values while mitigating risks. This comprehensive toolkit not only seeks to protect financial assets but also aims to enhance their potential for positive, sustainable impact. Such proactive and informed management empowers investors to contribute meaningfully to a more sustainable and equitable future.

Insurance and Sustainable Investing is an often-overlooked yet crucial component of managing risk in socially responsible investing. Navigating the world of sustainable investing means considering not only the potential for financial returns but also the underlying values that a portfolio represents. With this double bottom line in mind, the application of insurance strategies can be instrumental in protecting both capital and conscience. It serves as a safety net for investors who are keen to align their investments with their values without compromising on the security of their financial goals.

Insurance in the sustainable investing realm isn't just about safeguarding assets against the unforeseen. It's also about understanding how traditional insurance products can be leveraged to enhance a portfolio's resilience while maintaining a commitment to ethical and environmentally conscious practices. For instance, some insurers are pioneering products tailored to support sustainable initiatives, such as offering lower premiums for properties that meet certain green building standards. By choosing such policies, investors can manage risks effectively and promote their dedication to sustainability.

Delving into specifics, consider liability insurance for entities heavily involved in social impact. Companies that align deeply with social goals often face distinctive risks, including reputational risks that are harder to quantify but equally significant. By securing the right liability insurance, these businesses can mitigate the financial repercussions of potential backlash or litigation, ensuring that a single misstep doesn't erase years of positive impact.

Additionally, property and casualty insurance plays a pivotal role for investors who have large holdings in real assets geared towards sustainability, like renewable energy installations. These assets are susceptible to natural disasters that are exacerbated by climate change. Insurance solutions tailored to cover such occurrences not only safeguard the investments but also encourage continued investment in sectors critical for environmental sustainability. The insurance industry itself recognizes these shifts and is increasingly offering products that cater specifically to the green sector.

Consider the innovative insurance products arising from partnerships between insurers and sustainable finance experts. This collaboration is leading to the development of financial instruments like parametric insurance, which pays out automatically based on predetermined indicators rather than assessed damage. Such instruments are particularly useful in renewable energy sectors like wind farms or solar arrays, where quick recovery from weather-induced interruptions is crucial.

But insurance in this context is more than a defensive strategy. It's also about contributing positively to sustainable development. Insurers wield substantial influence in how capital is reallocated towards responsible enterprises by setting sustainability criteria for coverage. Their decisions are pivotal, as more underwriting companies choose to disassociate from industries like coal or support broader adaption strategies through resilience-building projects.

Furthermore, innovations in insurance investments themselves illustrate how the sector can galvanize the transition to a more sustainable future. Insurance companies, as significant investors, are beginning to integrate ESG factors into their portfolios, highlighting that they too face and address sustainability-related risk and opportunity. By integrating such factors, they're not just shielding their capital and clients—their choices help steer the broader market toward more sustainable practices.

On a personal investing level, insurance products aligned with ESG criteria can help individuals and small business owners align their policies with their values. For example, life insurance policies that invest the premiums in ESG-compliant portfolios give policyholders an additional layer to reflect their values, even in their insurance plans. This synergy between personal values and financial planning presents a holistic opportunity for individuals seeking sustainable lifestyles beyond direct investments.

Integrating insurance into sustainable investing strategies requires a nuanced understanding of both fields. Financial planners and wealth managers play a key role in this integration, advising clients on the types of insurance that best suit their sustainable investment portfolios. They ensure that clients are protected from unforeseen financial losses while considering the ethical implications of their coverage choices.

Ultimately, as the momentum of sustainable investing continues to grow, the insurance sector is set to become an even more intrinsic partner in this journey. The interplay between sustainability and insurance is challenging traditional boundaries, offering investors new approaches to manage risks effectively. As stakeholders increasingly demand transparency and responsibility, the insurance industry is well-positioned to influence outcomes positively, reinforcing sustainable practices while continuing to provide essential risk mitigation.

For any investor interested in sustainable investing, understanding how insurance can play a part in risk management is vital. With effective strategies and responsible choices, combining these fields will help navigate the complex landscape of risks within ESG investing, providing both protection and a promotion of values that echo through every financial decision.

Chapter 6:
Tax-Efficient Investing for Sustainability

Maximizing returns while championing sustainability isn't only about choosing the right investments; it also requires an astute understanding of tax implications. This means recognizing how tax-efficient strategies can bolster your commitment to sustainable investing. By thoughtfully selecting account types, such as tax-deferred or tax-exempt accounts, you can align your financial choices with sustainable values, potentially easing your tax burdens along the way. Moreover, incorporating strategic charitable giving can achieve dual objectives: it supports causes important to you and it offers tax benefits. Navigating the landscape of tax-efficient investing involves both a commitment to sustainable growth and an eye for fiscal prudence. With the right strategies in place, your sustainable investments can thrive fiscally while making a positive impact.

Tax Implications of Sustainable Investments Investing sustainably isn't just about aligning your values with your portfolio; it also involves navigating a complex web of tax considerations. Making sound decisions in this realm can be as crucial as picking the right assets. But what exactly are the tax implications that come with sustainable investments, and how can they affect your investment strategy?

Sustainable investments often include stocks, bonds, or funds that focus on environmental, social, and governance (ESG) criteria. These investments might be subject to different tax treatment depending on the structure of the investment itself. For example, green bonds, which are designed to finance projects with environmental benefits, may qualify for tax incentives in certain jurisdictions. Understanding these nuances can save an investor significant sums in annual tax liabilities.

Moreover, the investment structure plays a vital role. Long-term capital gains on stocks held for more than a year are typically taxed at a lower rate than short-term gains. This tax structure can encourage sustainable investors to hold their investments for longer periods, both supporting sustainable practices and potentially offering tax benefits. However, sustainable funds and ETFs might also generate short-term gains depending on their management and turnover, impacting your tax outcomes based on the fund's approach.

One tax advantage of incorporating ESG-focused investments is through tax-efficient accounts like IRAs or 401(k)s. These accounts allow you to defer taxes on earnings or, in some cases, receive tax-free distributions, thus enhancing the growth potential of your sustainable investments. Utilizing these accounts effectively requires understanding the rules governing contributions and withdrawals, which can vary based on the account type and age of the investor.

It is also worth noting the impact of dividends. Sustainable investments might yield dividends that offer different tax advantages. For example, qualified dividends from U.S.-based companies typically qualify for lower tax rates than ordinary income, again depending on the investor's holding period. An in-depth understanding of dividend classifications can lead to better tax optimization.

However, tax implications don't end with dividends and capital gains. Sustainable investments can also generate taxable events through activities such as corporate actions, mergers, and spin-offs, which might be prevalent in industries striving for sustainability transitions. Such events might alter the cost basis or require detailed tracking of investment adjustments.

The role of tax-loss harvesting shouldn't be overlooked either. This strategy can be effective in offsetting gains with losses to minimize the tax burden. Consider a scenario where an ESG fund underperforms; selling the investment strategically enables investors to capture losses while adhering to wash sale rules, all while maintaining an ESG-focused portfolio.

Additionally, sustainable investors might have the opportunity to leverage tax credits and deductions specific to renewable energy and sustainable practices. Investing in solar projects or energy efficiency can often provide direct tax incentives or credits, significantly influencing investment returns. While such opportunities are highly attractive, they require precise planning and awareness of evolving tax legislation.

On the broader spectrum, tax policy changes can significantly impact sustainable investing. Governments are increasingly acknowledging the need to promote sustainability through favorable tax regulations. Future policies might expand tax credits or deductions as incentives for sustainable projects. Therefore, staying informed about tax legislation and working with knowledgeable tax advisors is essential.

In closing, while sustainable investments offer abundant opportunities, they come with intricate tax considerations that require attention. Thoughtful planning, coupled with the strategic use of various investment accounts and tax strategies, can help maximize benefits. Balancing these aspects not only enhances financial returns but also strengthens commitment to sustainable practices, creating a ripple effect for broader societal change.

Account Types and Tax Efficiency Investing sustainably is a thoughtful journey, and at its heart lies the potent ability to fuse efficiency with impact. Understanding the impact of different account types on tax efficiency is crucial in this journey. Different account types serve varying purposes, and knowing which one optimizes tax efficiency can bolster your sustainable investing strategy.

When contemplating the intersection of account types and tax efficiency, the role of taxable brokerage accounts is pivotal. These accounts are flexible and accessible, allowing investors to buy and sell investments anytime. However, keep in mind the tax implications associated with capital gains. Realizing short-term gains, for instance, could result in paying a higher tax rate compared to long-term gains. Being mindful about the timing of selling assets or rebalancing your portfolio can help manage and minimize potential tax liabilities.

On the other hand, tax-advantaged accounts such as IRAs and 401(k)s are designed to enhance tax efficiency and long-term growth potential. Contributions to Traditional IRAs or 401(k)s are typically made with pre-tax dollars, lowering taxable income today. The growth within these accounts is tax-deferred, meaning it isn't subject to taxes until distributions are taken, ideally at a lower tax bracket in retirement. This tax deferral can significantly enhance the compounding effect over time.

Roth IRAs present a contrasting, yet complementary, angle on tax efficiency. Contributions to Roth IRAs are made with after-tax dollars, which implies that while you don't benefit from a tax deduction upfront, qualified withdrawals in retirement are tax-free. This can be particularly advantageous if you're anticipating being in a higher tax bracket upon retirement or if you expect substantial investment growth. The tax-free nature of these withdrawals can be strategically advantageous in a sustainable investing strategy, providing flexibility in managing taxable income in future life phases.

Furthermore, considering Health Savings Accounts (HSAs) can also promote tax efficiency. Although HSAs are primarily earmarked for healthcare expenses, they offer a unique triple tax advantage. Contributions are tax-deductible, and the investment growth within the account, much like Roth IRAs, is tax-free as long as distributions are used for qualified medical expenses. For sustainably-focused individuals, HSAs still offer investment choices that align with ESG values, therefore enhancing tax strategy while adhering to personal principles.

Tax efficiency can also be achieved through tax-loss harvesting— an essential technique in managing taxable accounts. By offsetting gains with losses, you can reduce taxable income. This strategy is especially effective in volatile markets, where fluctuations present opportunities to capture losses without altering the overall strategic asset allocation. Such techniques can help in preserving capital while maintaining a commitment to sustainability.

Another tactic to consider is the use of tax-efficient mutual funds or ETFs, which are designed to minimize taxable distributions. These funds adopt strategies like low turnover or loss harvesting within the fund itself, aspiring to distribute fewer capital gains to shareholders. In sustainably-focused portfolios, such vehicles can be particularly attractive, offering both the benefit of low costs and adherence to ESG principles.

However, it's not just about the type of account you choose; it's also about strategic asset placement. By placing frequently traded or income-generating assets like bonds in tax-advantaged accounts and keeping tax-efficient investments like index funds or ETFs in taxable accounts, you can effectively enhance overall tax efficiency. This strategy also leverages the differential tax treatment of various income types, proving beneficial for long-term accumulation.

It's worth noting that engaging with financial advisors knowledgeable about tax-efficient strategies and sustainable investing can significantly improve outcomes. Their expertise, especially in navigating the complexities of tax codes and investment vehicles, is invaluable. Furthermore, they can offer customized strategies that match your unique financial goals, risk tolerance, and sustainability ethos, reflecting a thoroughly tailored approach to investing.

In the grand scheme, upholding a balance between sustainability and tax efficiency requires continuous learning and adaptation. The landscape of both investing and taxation is dynamic, with laws and conditions evolving over time. Regularly reviewing account types, staying informed about potential tax law changes, and adjusting strategies accordingly is crucial to maintaining tax efficiency.

To sum up, selecting the appropriate account types forms the bedrock of optimizing tax efficiency in sustainable investing. Whether it's leveraging the tax advantages of retirement accounts, executing strategic asset placement, or engaging in tax-loss harvesting, each element plays a pivotal role in shaping a holistic, effective strategy. By weaving these aspects into your sustainable investment narrative, you're not only aligning actions with your values but also fortifying your financial future. As we advance, remember that your commitment to learning, adapting, and passionately pursuing financial wisdom is your strongest ally.

Charitable Giving Strategies in sustainable investing can be an effective approach to aligning your financial goals with your values. When done thoughtfully, it helps maximize the impact of your generosity while providing potential tax benefits. Charitable giving in the context of sustainable investing doesn't just mean writing a check. It involves a deliberate strategy that's woven into your overall portfolio design and financial plan.

First, let's explore some key reasons why charitable giving should be part of your sustainable investing strategy. By integrating philanthropy, you're not just fostering a legacy of financial support, but also influencing organizations and projects that align with your personal values. This can range from supporting renewable energy projects to funding social enterprises that drive positive change.

One effective strategy is to focus on *donor-advised funds (DAFs)*, which have become increasingly popular among values-driven investors. A DAF allows you to make a charitable donation, receive a tax deduction, and then recommend grants to charities of your choice over time. This provides both immediate tax efficiency and the flexibility to align grant recommendations with your evolving values and investment goals.

Another approach is using appreciated securities for charitable giving. Donating stock that's gone up in value since you purchased it can significantly increase your tax savings. When you donate appreciated securities, you're not just avoiding capital gains tax, you're also receiving a deduction for the full market value of the donated stock. This method allows you to give more to your chosen causes without impacting your cash flow, ultimately increasing your philanthropic impact.

Additionally, consider establishing a charitable remainder trust (CRT). CRTs can be designed to provide an income stream for yourself or other beneficiaries for a specified period, with the remainder going to charity. They offer a range of tax benefits, including a partial charitable deduction and the potential to defer or even avoid capital gains tax on the sale of appreciated assets. CRTs are an excellent option for those interested in blending philanthropy with financial planning.

For families, involving future generations in charitable planning can multiply both impact and engagement. Young people often bring fresh perspectives and energy to philanthropic discussions, fostering a shared commitment to sustainable investment goals. This intergenerational involvement not only strengthens family bonds but ensures that family philanthropies continue to reflect shared values over time.

It's important to consider the timing of your charitable contributions as well, especially for those looking to optimize tax efficiency. For instance, bunching deductions—by concentrating charitable contributions in a single year—can help maximize tax benefits by allowing a taxpayer to exceed the standard deduction threshold.

You'll want to work closely with your financial planner and tax advisor to ensure your charitable giving aligns with your comprehensive financial strategy. These professionals can help tailor your giving approach to suit your unique tax situation and make sure that it complements other components of your sustainable investment plan. With skilled guidance, you can pinpoint not just where your money should go, but also how giving can enhance your overall financial well-being.

Let's take a closer look at impact investing as part of your charitable giving strategy. This approach allows you to invest in companies, organizations, and funds with the mission of generating measurable social and environmental impacts alongside financial returns. Impact investing enables you to fulfill charitable objectives while maintaining the potential for capital appreciation, thus integrating seamlessly with both your giving goals and investment strategy.

Grammar and syntax aside, the ripple effect of charitable giving within sustainable investing is profound. By targeting industries and innovations that tackle pressing issues like climate change, poverty, and inequality, you're not just supporting these causes; you're empowering them to grow, flourish, and create lasting change on a grand scale.

Lastly, remember that sustainable charitable giving should be a journey, not a destination. As markets, regulations, and personal circumstances change, so too should your giving strategy. Regularly review your approach to ensure it continues to align with your values and objectives. Engage with the charities and causes you support to see the tangible impacts of your contributions and recalibrate your strategy if necessary.

In the end, employing strategic charitable giving within the context of a sustainable investment portfolio isn't just about the immediate benefits—it's about crafting a legacy. It's about setting the foundation for a path where financial success and positive social influence coexist. And that's a vision worth pursuing.

Chapter 7:
Sustainable Retirement Planning

As you steer toward the horizon of retirement, sustaining your lifestyle in alignment with your values becomes paramount. Sustainable retirement planning isn't just about amassing wealth; it's about investing in a future that resonates with your principles. By intertwining retirement goals with sustainable investments, you can ensure your nest egg isn't just financially robust but also conscientious. Socially responsible retirement accounts offer options that match ethical standards with financial needs, providing satisfaction in both growth and impact. Crafting a distribution strategy that reflects your values lets you leave a lasting mark, reinforcing that your financial decisions contribute positively to society and the environment. This fusion of ethics and finances doesn't just prepare you for retirement— it's a pledge to further positive change, ensuring that your golden years truly embody the legacy you wish to leave behind.

Aligning Your Retirement Goals with Sustainable Investments begins by recognizing that retirement planning involves more than just financial preparation; it's about aligning your long-term financial security with your personal values. In recent years, sustainable investments have emerged as a powerful way to merge these two objectives. Whether you're an individual investor crafting your retirement strategy or a financial planner guiding others, sustainable investments offer a way to champion environmental, social, and governance (ESG) principles while ensuring a secure future.

What does it mean to align your retirement goals with sustainable investments? It's about integrating values such as social responsibility, environmental stewardship, and corporate governance into your financial decisions. As you chart your path to retirement, consider the impact you want your investments to make. This alignment isn't just about feeling good; it also plays a crucial role in the longevity and stability of your portfolio.

Investments that prioritize ESG criteria have shown resilience in the face of market volatility. For many, sustainable investments represent an opportunity to perform well financially while also doing good in the world. This dual benefit becomes particularly appealing when planning for retirement, as it supports long-term wealth creation and ethical considerations.

Sustainable investing isn't a one-size-fits-all approach, so it's essential to define what sustainability means for you personally. Do you value environmental conservation more than corporate governance, or is social impact your top priority? Sorting these priorities helps determine which ESG factors will drive your investment decisions. With the increasing number of investment products dedicated to responsible investing, you can customize your portfolio to reflect these personal values.

To effectively align your retirement goals with sustainable investments, start by reviewing your current portfolio. Are your existing investments aligned with your ethical standards? Conduct a thorough ESG assessment to evaluate where changes are necessary to meet your alignment objectives. A shift towards more sustainable assets can sometimes require re-evaluation of traditional assets, considering factors such as carbon emissions or human rights records.

One strategy for aligning your goals with sustainable methods is to identify specific ESG-related funds or securities. Numerous mutual funds and exchange-traded funds (ETFs) now focus exclusively on

ESG metrics, making it easier than ever to integrate sustainable options into your portfolio. These funds often rigorously screen for companies meeting high standards of ethical practice, environmental impact, and transparent governance.

Another practical approach includes using sustainable indexes as benchmarks. They offer a clearer perspective on how different ESG-focused assets perform over time. By utilizing this data, you can make informed decisions that align with both your ethical and financial expectations for retirement.

Engagement is key. Monitoring companies' performance in ESG areas allows you to remain vigilant and active in your investment choices. Participation in shareholder meetings and voting on sustainability resolutions can further influence corporate behavior towards more ethical practices, cultivating a positive feedback loop that benefits society and your investments.

When aligning your retirement goals with sustainable investments, don't neglect risk assessment. Sustainable investments come with their unique set of risks, including market volatility and regulatory shifts. However, having a diversified portfolio with a balance of ESG-focused assets can mitigate many of these concerns. The aim is to balance achieving your financial retirement goals with contributing positively to societal challenges.

Furthermore, consider the potential tax benefits of sustainable investments. Retirement accounts such as IRAs or 401(k)s can be structured to include sustainable options, providing tax-efficient avenues for growing your portfolio with an eye on ESG criteria. Consult with a financial advisor who specializes in sustainable investments to explore these options fully.

As you align your retirement plans with sustainable investments, it's essential to communicate these objectives with your family or heirs.

By doing so, you ensure your values and financial intentions are understood and preserved beyond your lifetime. This process of legacy planning solidifies the impact of your ESG investments for future generations to appreciate and build upon.

Ultimately, aligning your retirement goals with sustainable investments is a dynamic and rewarding endeavor that requires thoughtful consideration, ongoing education, and adaptability. As the world continuously evolves, so too do the opportunities to make meaningful investment choices that reflect your ethos and secure your future. In embracing this alignment, you not only pave the way for a financially stable retirement but also contribute toward a more sustainable planet.

Socially Responsible Retirement Accounts are an increasingly important component of sustainable retirement planning. Within the realm of investing, aligning financial goals with personal ethics can be both rewarding and challenging. For many investors, the journey to preserving wealth is deeply intertwined with the desire to do good in the world. Socially responsible retirement accounts provide a structured pathway for achieving these dual objectives and are becoming a focal point for investors who value sustainability alongside financial growth.

At the core of socially responsible retirement accounts is the integration of Environmental, Social, and Governance (ESG) criteria into traditional retirement planning methods. By weaving these considerations into investment decisions, individuals can ensure their retirement savings contribute positively to society while still working to secure a comfortable future. Unlike the conventional approaches to retirement planning that often emphasize short-term financial gains, socially responsible accounts focus on long-term value creation, considering the broader impact of investments on society and the planet.

To truly benefit from this approach, investors need to take a comprehensive look at their existing retirement accounts such as 401(k)s, IRAs, and Roth IRAs. Many employers now offer ESG options within their retirement plans. Those managing their own retirement funds can seek out mutual funds, ETFs, and other financial instruments that adhere to socially responsible principles. It's crucial to understand the nuances of these options, including any potential trade-offs in terms of costs, risks, and returns.

Adopting a socially responsible strategy often begins with understanding the values that matter most to you. For some, it's about reducing carbon footprints or supporting companies with progressive diversity policies. Others might focus on corporate governance or labor rights. Once clear on personal values, investors can choose funds and account types that align with these priorities. Various investment platforms and tools now offer screens to help filter investments based on specific ESG criteria, making the process more accessible than ever before.

Socially responsible investing is not merely a trend but a fundamental shift in the way individuals and institutions think about future security and societal well-being. As the demand for sustainable retirement options continues to grow, the financial industry is responding with a broader array of products and services. Innovations in fintech and a deeper focus on ESG disclosures are pivotal to facilitating more informed and impactful investment decisions.

While the idea of tailoring retirement accounts to social causes is appealing, scrutinizing the authenticity of ESG claims is paramount. The risk of greenwashing—where funds present themselves as socially responsible without substantial backing—is real. Investors should conduct thorough research or consult with knowledgeable financial advisors to discern genuine ESG offerings. Evaluating a fund's historical performance on ESG issues alongside its financial returns can provide clarity and confidence in investment choices.

One way to reinforce the integrity of socially responsible retirement accounts is through active ownership and shareholder advocacy. Investors, collectively or individually, can influence corporate behaviors by voting on shareholder resolutions and engaging with company management. This role as active stewards of capital empowers investors to advocate for specific environmental innovations or social reforms within the companies they invest in.

Another key consideration for these types of retirement accounts is their compatibility with individual's risk tolerance and time horizon. Often, socially responsible investments require patience as they typically prioritize ethical outcomes and sustainable practices, which may yield competitive returns over the long haul rather than immediate gains. Understanding this dynamic helps set appropriate expectations and aligns financial strategies with personal convictions.

Tax-efficiency also plays an integral role in maximizing the benefits of socially responsible retirement accounts. Certain account structures allow for advantageous tax treatment, supporting the responsible allocation of assets without eroding their value through excessive taxation. Strategies such as funding retirement accounts with pre-tax contributions, leveraging Roth conversions, and using tax-loss harvesting can enhance the financial effectiveness of socially responsible investing.

Moreover, combining socially responsible retirement planning with charitable giving strategies can amplify both impact and tax benefits. Investors might consider incorporating donor-advised funds or charitable remainder trusts into their retirement plans. These options can provide dual benefits of achieving philanthropic goals while enjoying potential tax advantages and income streams during retirement.

Ultimately, the journey of integrating socially responsible accounts into retirement planning is deeply personal and reflective of a commitment to harmonize financial success with ethical integrity. It involves not just a shift in financial strategy but also a transformation in mindset—moving beyond traditional metrics of success and embracing a holistic view that encompasses both personal well-being and societal impact.

In summary, Socially Responsible Retirement Accounts provide a compelling blueprint for investors seeking to sustain both their finances and the world around them. By embedding ethical considerations into retirement plans, individuals can influence positive change while working towards their own financial security. As more tools and resources become available, the path to sustainable retirement planning becomes clearer and more attainable for all. The end result is a retirement strategy that not only supports a comfortable lifestyle but also leaves a lasting, positive imprint on the world.

Retirement Distribution Strategies That Reflect Your Values are an essential part of sustainable retirement planning. When you think about the future, it's not just about putting enough money aside to live comfortably; it's about ensuring your money continues to work in ways that align with your core beliefs. The choices you make about distributing your retirement savings can impact not only your lifestyle but also the world around you. This alignment can be deeply satisfying as it lets you blend financial prudence with personal ethics.

First and foremost, it's crucial to recognize that retirement distribution is more than just a financial decision; it's about expressing your values through economic power. Crafting a distribution strategy that respects your principles involves identifying what causes or concerns resonate most with you. Whether it's environmental sustainability, social justice, or ethical governance, these factors should guide how you allocate your resources post-retirement. By carefully selecting financial products and charitable options that reflect your values, you effectively extend the impact of your life's work beyond your own household.

Your distribution strategy can also reflect your values through the choice of where you hold your retirement accounts. Socially responsible retirement accounts, like those that include ESG-screened funds, allow you to invest in assets that don't just promise financial returns but also contribute positively to societal goals. It's worth consulting with your financial advisor to understand the performance and fees associated with such accounts, as they may differ from traditional investment options. Ensuring that your money supports ethical companies reinforces the principles you've lived by throughout your career, transforming retirement planning into a testament to those values.

An often-overlooked aspect of retirement planning is the way you withdraw your funds. Implementing a systematic withdrawal strategy that minimizes tax implications can release more capital for ethical investments or charitable contributions. Living off interest rather than principal, or following withdrawal rules that align with the required minimum distribution (RMD) guidelines, ensures the longest possible lifespan for your ethical investments. By maximizing what you withdraw without negatively impacting your portfolio's longevity or ethical contributions, you guard both your finances and values into the future.

Philanthropy is another powerful tool to consider when integrating your values into retirement distribution. Whether you set up a donor-advised fund or make direct contributions to causes you support, using a portion of your post-retirement assets for charitable giving can leave a lasting legacy. This is not just about monetary contribution; it's a way of influencing the world and showing gratitude for the opportunities you've been afforded. Planned giving can be strategized to ensure the greatest impact, both for the beneficiaries and your tax responsibilities.

Moreover, embracing green energy investments as part of your retirement distribution strategy reinforces commitment to sustainability. If you're passionate about environmental causes, directing your money towards renewable energy or green bonds can be highly effective. These investments not only support the fight against climate change but also have the potential for fulfilling returns. Aligning your distribution choices with your ecofriendly values makes your retirement savings work beyond conventional bounds and promotes a healthier planet.

Estate planning offers yet another avenue to reflect your values post-retirement. While many view estate planning as a means to pass wealth to the next generation, it can also involve establishing trusts or foundations focused on sustainable initiatives. This approach ensures that your legacy continues to fund world-changing projects and instills these values in your descendants. By structuring your estate to reflect your ethics, you offer the gift of values-driven wealth to those who follow in your footsteps.

The decisions you make about distributing your assets during retirement should involve more than financial projections; they should be guided by a comprehensive understanding of what you stand for. As you make these decisions, consider incorporating input from family members or a trusted financial advisor who shares your commitment to sustainability. Open dialogues about ethical pursuits and shared values can lead to strategic decisions that honor your ideals.

Instituting retirement distribution strategies that reflect your values requires thoughtful planning and proactive engagement with both the financial and ethical aspects. By aligning your retirement methods with the beliefs you've held close throughout life, you turn financial planning into a profound reflection of your identity. This conscious effort helps ensure that your influence persists, supporting a world that better mirrors the ideals you cherish. As you navigate this path, take comfort in knowing that your savings and investments are contributing to a future you can be proud of, long after you have retired.

Chapter 8:
Estate Planning with a Conscience

As we transition into the realm of estate planning, it's time to consider how your legacy can leave a meaningful impact aligned with your personal values. Estate planning with a conscience means more than just distributing assets; it's about integrating your sustainable and ethical values into the future welfare of generations to come. Whether through thoughtful trust structures or establishing foundations that carry your philanthropic beliefs forward, conscientious estate planning offers a way to perpetuate the positive changes you've championed in life. It's an opportunity to instill your values in your descendants, ensuring they embrace both financial acumen and social responsibility. Educating future generations about ethical wealth management not only prepares them for a sound financial future but also empowers them to become stewards of positive change. Taking these steps ensures your life's work continues to make a difference, long after you've passed it on. Embrace the chance to craft an enduring legacy that reflects who you are and what you stand for—a legacy of both fiscal wisdom and profound ethical influence.

Incorporating Sustainable Values in Your Estate Planning
We live in a world where sustainability isn't just a buzzword—it's a guiding principle for many. As you plan your estate, it's crucial to incorporate sustainable values that reflect your legacy and principles. A sustainable estate plan not only ensures the continued stewardship of your assets but also models conscientious living for generations to

come. Let's delve into how you can weave sustainability into your estate plan while aligning with broader financial goals.

First things first, understanding the concept of sustainability in estate planning involves looking beyond mere wealth transfer. It's about ensuring that the resources and values you hold dear are passed on in a way that respects the environment, benefits society, and maintains economic strength. This approach doesn't just take into account monetary assets; it includes the preservation of land, investments in sustainable businesses, and support for charitable causes.

One effective way to integrate your sustainable values into an estate plan is by setting clear intentions for your assets. Specify how you'd like your wealth to be used, particularly if it's tied to sustainable or ethical causes. For instance, if you're passionate about combating climate change, consider earmarking funds for renewable energy projects or conservation efforts. This isn't just about checking a box; it's about making a genuine impact.

Another key component is the use of trusts and foundations. These tools can effectively manage and distribute your assets according to your ethical beliefs. By establishing a trust with sustainable mandates, you ensure that your legacy doesn't just fade over time. Instead, it grows, nurturing causes that matter to you. Trusts can include stipulations for socially responsible investing, so they're aligned with ESG (Environmental, Social, Governance) criteria, which is increasingly becoming a standard in conscientious financial management.

Moreover, when structuring your estate, consider the potential tax benefits that come with sustainable investing and charitable giving. Various jurisdictions offer tax incentives for green investments and contributions to non-profits. By leveraging these incentives, you not only align your estate with your values but also increase the overall impact by minimizing tax liabilities. A well-informed financial planner or tax advisor can guide you through these nuances to maximize benefits.

Thinking about the future generations is also pivotal. Sustainable estate planning is as much about empowering your heirs as it is about asset distribution. Educate your family on the importance of maintaining sustainability in their financial decisions. This educational element ensures that the values you hold dear don't simply exist as legal stipulations in a document but as lived experiences that inspire and guide your descendants. Something you can do is set aside funds specifically for education or training in fields such as environmental science or social entrepreneurship, encouraging family members to actively participate in sustainable practices.

Don't overlook the power of philanthropy. Directing part of your estate toward philanthropic endeavors is one of the most effective ways to leave a lasting impact. This could be done through bequests to charitable organizations or creating a family foundation focused on causes close to your heart. It's a definitive statement that your life's work is about more than accumulation—it's about meaningful contribution and change.

Investments can also be aligned with sustainable principles through what you might call "impact investments." These are investments made with the intention of generating a measurable, beneficial social or environmental impact alongside a financial return. Incorporating these into your estate plan—whether during your lifetime or through instructions in your will—ensures your capital is actively working for good. Your legacy could quite literally be the wind at the back of innovation in renewable energy or sustainable agriculture.

A growing trend is ethical wills, which are not legally binding but serve as a heartfelt document sharing your values, guiding principles, and hopes for future generations. This intentional communication complements your formal estate plan and emphasizes your commitment to sustainable values. It's a deeply personal way to share lessons learned, dreams for the future, and express why sustainability is foundational to your planning.

While numbers and documents are essential, stories and values are what truly bind us. As you establish your estate plan, think of yourself as a steward who brings others along on this journey toward a more sustainable future. This requires ongoing engagement, where you review and adapt your plans in conjunction with ever-evolving socio-economic dynamics and personal circumstances. You might think of your estate plan as a living document, one that grows and changes just as you do.

Finally, remember that estate planning, like sustainability itself, is not a one-time task but a dynamic process. Regularly reviewing and updating your plan ensures it reflects any shifts in your values or priorities and responds to changes in your family's situation, the market, and societal needs. The result is a holistic estate plan that is not just about what you leave behind, but what you contribute to the world. It's about crafting a legacy that truly embodies your lifetime of passions, principles, and purpose.

Trusts and Foundations for Sustainable Wealth Transfer play a pivotal role in bridging the gap between today's responsible stewardship and tomorrow's impactful legacy. When you're considering how to pass on your wealth, think not just about the mechanics of the transfer but also the values and principles embedded in your estate plan. Creating a structure that ensures your philanthropic goals and sustainable ambitions are adhered to can be both empowering and challenging.

Trusts have been a cornerstone of estate planning for centuries, providing a flexible vehicle for asset management and distribution.

Traditional trusts can be structured to support your sustainable values by embedding specific provisions that compel trustees to invest in socially responsible ways. This could mean stipulating that trust assets must be invested in funds that prioritize environmental sustainability, social responsibility, or corporate governance excellence.

But how do you ensure these values aren't just a footnote, but rather a central theme of your trust? It starts with clarity and intention. Clearly define the purpose of the trust — whether it's preserving capital, supporting a philanthropic cause, or providing education for future generations. Then, integrate ESG criteria as essential investment directives. This might involve selecting trustees who share your sustainable vision or engaging third-party advisors specializing in ESG investments to guide your portfolio choices.

Foundations, on the other hand, offer a structured platform to perpetuate charitable giving aligned with your ethos. When you create a foundation, you're establishing more than just a financial repository; you're crafting an enduring impact on societal issues that matter to you. Unlike a trust, a foundation often has a broader mandate for community engagement, enabling you to back initiatives with both financial resources and active advocacy.

One strategy is to establish a private foundation, enabling you and your family to maintain control over investment decisions and grant distributions. This control allows your foundation to not only support projects aligned with your values but also financially sustain itself through return-generating, mission-aligned investments. Foundations can incorporate practices such as impact investing or program-related investments, directing funds towards enterprises that are both financially viable and socially beneficial.

In implementing these vehicles, it's essential to balance pragmatism with passion. An overly ambitious mandate might stretch resources too thin or lack focus, while overly rigid constraints could stifle innovation and adaptability. Engage with professional advisors to ensure that the trust or foundation is structured to achieve optimal tax efficiencies and compliance with legal frameworks, while still adhering to the sustainable principles that are close to your heart.

The beauty of these instruments lies in their ability to scale with your vision. Trusts can support the education and financial wellbeing of your grandchildren, while a foundation's resources might help chip away at global issues like poverty or climate change. They're not just mechanisms for wealth transfer but powerful tools for sustaining and amplifying your values over time.

Consider too the educational component. As you plan, involve your children and perhaps even your grandchildren in discussions about the trust or foundation's purpose and objectives. This involvement can serve a dual purpose: fostering generational cohesion around shared values and preparing heirs to manage these vehicles responsibly. By educating the next generation about the importance of sustainable investing and philanthropy, you plant the seeds for a perpetuating cycle of conscious wealth stewardship.

You might also explore collaborative foundations which pool resources for greater impact, aligning with other like-minded donors to tackle issues that are close to your collective hearts. This approach not only multiplies the financial contribution but can also leverage diverse perspectives and networks, driving more innovative solutions.

It's no small task creating a legacy that endures. Yet, with trusts and foundations tailored to your vision, you can set a powerful precedent for financial stewardship that not only honors your values but also elevates the philanthropies, communities, and causes that matter most. This intentional alignment of wealth transfer with sustainability establishes a profound and lasting impact, echoing through the generations.

Ultimately, when you align your estate planning with your conscience through these instruments, you're not just transferring wealth — you're transferring wisdom, principles, and a sustainable worldview that will inspire and enrich countless lives.

Generational Financial Education and Legacy involves more than just passing on assets; it's about ensuring the values and principles that guided your financial decisions resonate through future generations. Estate planning with a conscience isn't just a checklist of assets to be distributed; it's a thoughtful exercise in aligning your legacies with the principles of sustainability, ethics, and fiscal responsibility. Such planning requires intentional efforts not only to secure financial stability but also to inculcate financial literacy and responsible stewardship in heirs.

Creating a legacy involves a dual mandate: managing wealth effectively and imparting financial wisdom. The evolution of your estate plan into a learning tool for your family can be fulfilling. It begins with engaging conversations about the family's history, core values, and the purpose of wealth. These dialogues foster a sense of shared responsibility and clarify the purpose of the wealth being passed on—whether it's supporting charitable causes, advancing education, or sustaining family businesses.

Financial education is a critical aspect that cannot be overlooked. Equipping the next generation with the skills they need to understand, manage, and grow their inherited wealth ensures they don't feel overwhelmed. Implementing educational programs and workshops tailored to the family's specific values and goals can enhance comprehension. These sessions could range from understanding the basics of investing and the significance of sustainable investing to more complex topics like estate tax strategies and trust management.

Inclusive family meetings are powerful platforms for open discussions, encouraging transparency and reducing conflicts.

Involving younger generations in the decision-making process can cultivate a sense of ownership and responsibility. Let them express what sustainability means to them personally and explore how it can reflect in future investment and philanthropic endeavors. When they see themselves as active participants rather than passive recipients, they're more likely to honor the family's conscientious objectives.

The strategy might include setting up family councils or boards, where roles and responsibilities are designated, allowing everyone to have a voice and a stake in managing the estate. These councils can serve not only as governance bodies but also as educational environments where members learn by doing. An interactive approach to financial management encourages learning from peers and mentors both within and outside the family.

Incorporating sustainable practices into the family's financial planning isn't just about changing the portfolio; it's about exemplifying a commitment to the environment and society through every financial decision made. Teaching this commitment through personal examples can be one of the most profound forms of education, reinforcing lessons in decision-making that prioritize long-term impacts over short-term gains.

Furthermore, technological advancements provide new platforms for financial education, offering online courses and digital resources that cater to various learning styles. Tailored content that highlights conscientious finance avenues can empower younger family members to explore their financial ethos without feeling overwhelmed by technical jargon. Providing continuous access to these tools is key, as continuous education should be a cornerstone of your legacy plan.

Trusts and foundations often play an integral role in legacy planning, serving dual roles as financial vehicles and educational tools. This isn't simply about creating safety nets but extending philanthropic legacies that can inspire and motivate future generations.

Comprehensive development of these entities should involve input from future beneficiaries, educating them on governance and the social objectives these structures aim to fulfill.

Establishing criteria for phased inheritance and involving heirs in the decision-making can align wealth transfer with financial maturity, ensuring they are prepared both mentally and financially to handle the responsibilities that come with wealth. Programs that measure readiness through specific benchmarks of financial competence could be implemented to ensure the heirs are well-prepared.

A key element of generational planning is the notion of stewardship over ownership. Teaching heirs the principles of stewardship imbues a deeper understanding of the social, environmental, and economic impacts of financial decisions. It's about ensuring heirs see themselves as caretakers of wealth, committed to maintaining and growing it responsibly for future generations and societal good.

It's imperative that the framework you've built in your life reflects in the legacy you leave behind. This involves steering clear of presumptions that wealth will automatically be a force for good. Active efforts and consistent education ensure that every dollar not only has a purpose but echoes the values and intentions set forth in your lifetime.

As you mold a financially literate, conscientious successor generation, you create a legacy that transcends material assets. This legacy becomes a testament to the values you've embodied and the change you've aspired to create. The intention behind every education initiative is to form not just savers and investors, but stewards and leaders attuned to the socio-economic fabrics that bind us all.

Chapter 9:
Selecting Sustainable Investments

As we dive into selecting sustainable investments, it's crucial to understand the intricacies of this dynamic landscape. The aim is to align your portfolio with investments that not only promise financial growth but also champion environmental, social, and governance (ESG) principles. You'll want to conduct thorough due diligence to ensure the authenticity and impact of potential ESG investments. Don't just chase trends—look for genuine opportunities like impact investing, where capital is directed towards generating measurable social and environmental benefits, or community investing, which empowers local economies and fosters sustainable development. Consider diversifying with green bonds or renewable energy projects as they offer a dual promise of potential returns and positive change. The key is not just to invest, but to invest with purpose, crafting a portfolio that reflects your values and contributes to a brighter, more sustainable future.

Due Diligence for ESG Investments demands a conscientious approach that aligns with your financial goals and ethical values. Navigating this realm requires a deep understanding of Environmental, Social, and Governance (ESG) factors, as these elements form the backbone of sustainable investing. But why is due diligence so crucial in ESG investments? Simple: it's about ensuring the commitments made by companies are genuine and not mere lip service.

Investors are often drawn to ESG investments because of the potential to enact positive change while achieving financial growth. However, not all that glitters is green. Some companies may engage in "greenwashing," making misleading claims about their environmental practices to attract ethical investors. Performing due diligence helps you cut through the noise, ensuring that your investment truly supports your values. Moreover, such investigation isn't just about verification. It's about aligning your investments with a broader vision of sustainability and ethical responsibility.

So, where do you begin? Start by examining the company's ESG policies and practices. Detailed reports and ratings can be a good starting point but don't stop there. Dig deeper into the specifics: Are the company's sustainability goals ambitious yet achievable? What concrete steps are they taking to reach them? Look for transparency in their reporting. Companies committed to ESG principles should provide clear, detailed, and regular updates on their progress. This openness is a good indicator of genuine commitment.

Consider the governance part of ESG very seriously. How diverse is the company's leadership? Diversity in leadership often translates to a broader perspective on social and environmental issues, and companies with diverse boards may be better positioned to handle the nuances of ESG investing. Furthermore, does the company have a history of regulatory issues or scandals? The answers may shed light on potential risks and alignments with your values.

An integral part of due diligence is assessing a company's environmental impact and commitments. Investigate how they manage resources, energy consumption, and waste. Are they pioneers in innovative technologies that reduce environmental harm? A company's carbon footprint, energy management, and even efforts in biodiversity conservation can be strong indicators of its environmental dedication. Contrast these against industry standards to assess relative performance instead of relying solely on absolute figures.

Social responsibility—another key component of ESG—is equally important. This includes how a company engages with its workforce, supply chain, and communities. Are labor practices ethical and fair? Does the company take steps to ensure social justice, equity, and inclusion? Labor strikes, lawsuits, or negative press can be red flags, suggesting the need for caution or further exploration. Additionally, how does the company contribute to community development and well-being? Corporate social responsibility programs that focus on education, health, or local initiatives can demonstrate a company's social commitment.

To effectively assess these elements, leverage the wealth of available resources and tools. ESG ratings by established agencies can offer valuable insights, but remember: they should only be part of your evaluation process. Use due diligence to interpret scores and consider why different agencies might offer different perspectives. Each agency has unique methodologies, strengths, and biases which can influence scores. Understanding these can help you make more informed decisions.

There's also intrinsic value in consulting annual reports and sustainability reports published by companies, as these documents often provide a comprehensive overview of their ESG strategies and achievements. Furthermore, shareholder meetings and announcements can offer critical insights into management's priorities and views on sustainability.

By putting in the work for rigorous due diligence, you empower yourself to build a portfolio that genuinely reflects your values and aspirations. Effective due diligence guides you in selecting companies that not only talk the talk but walk the walk regarding sustainable practices. As new ESG standards and regulations take shape, staying updated remains vital.

The journey toward mastering ESG investments through due diligence is like craftwork—requiring patience, skill, and an eye for detail. Your diligence here not only safeguards against potential risks but fundamentally enriches your investment strategy by ensuring it is ethically sound and aligned with your vision of a better world. With each step, you're closer to making a meaningful impact while securing your financial future.

Impact Investing and Community Investing Options fall under the broader umbrella of sustainable investment strategies, each offering unique avenues for aligning personal values with financial goals. Impact investing specifically aims to generate measurable social and environmental impacts alongside a financial return. It's an approach that goes beyond traditional investing by seeking to address issues such as climate change, poverty, and equality through investment choices. This investment strategy is compelling for those who wish to create tangible positive impacts while also building wealth.

Community investing, meanwhile, focuses on directing capital to underserved communities both in the U.S. and globally. It provides individuals, families, and businesses with opportunities to break the cycle of poverty by improving local infrastructure, creating jobs, and boosting economic development. Community investments might fund things like affordable housing projects, local businesses, or community banks that serve minority or low-income populations. By supporting enterprises that might otherwise lack access to capital, community investors are often directly contributing to societal equity and inclusion.

Both impact and community investing stem from a desire to do good while doing well. But to be truly effective, investors need to clearly define what "impact" means to them. For some, it might mean environmental stewardship, such as investing in renewable energy or sustainable agriculture. Others might focus more on social equity, favoring initiatives that improve access to education or healthcare. The beauty of impact investing lies in its flexibility and range of options, allowing investors to tailor their portfolios to reflect their personal convictions and long-term aspirations.

Making sense of these options can be overwhelming, particularly for those new to the concept. That's where the role of due diligence becomes imperative. Investors should consider several factors to ensure they're making informed choices. Key to this process is assessing the credibility of investment opportunities. Are the projects or companies truly committed to driving social or environmental change? Evaluate their fulfillment of promises and transparency in communication. Utilizing third-party assessments or reports can provide an additional layer of assurance and validation.

Furthermore, impact investing is not restricted to equities or funds. Green bonds, social bonds, and other fixed-income instruments also present viable avenues for conscientious investors. These bonds fund projects with both a financial return and a societal benefit — aspects we'll dive deeper into elsewhere in this book. An understanding of different asset classes helps create a diversified portfolio aligned with one's ethical focus. Moreover, they offer a degree of predictability and lower perceived risk, which can be especially appealing to those nearing retirement or with lower risk tolerance.

Case studies and success stories play a powerful role in illustrating the potential of impact and community investing. Consider initiatives that have turned around rural communities through microfinancing or loans that allowed small entrepreneurs to start businesses, hire employees, and contribute to local economies. Showing real-world examples where investments have resulted in cleaner energy systems or expanded educational opportunities helps underscore the tangible difference these strategies can make. These stories motivate and inspire, giving concrete evidence that investing with a conscience is not merely a trend but a viable financial strategy.

To maximize the effectiveness of impact and community investing, collaboration and partnerships are crucial. Whether it's connecting with other like-minded investors or partnering with nonprofits and governmental organizations, pooling resources and expertise can amplify impact. Shared efforts can lead to more significant, more scalable solutions, allowing for systemic changes that tackle root causes rather than merely addressing symptoms. Knowing where to find these partnerships and how to leverage them creates a comprehensive plan that aligns with both financial and philanthropic goals.

Measuring the success of impact investments is essential yet complex. Investors should employ a mix of qualitative and quantitative tools to gauge their contributions accurately. Look beyond traditional financial metrics — consider factors like social return on investment (SROI) or environmental impact assessments. Incorporating these evaluations provides a holistic view of how well investments are meeting their intended objectives. Not only does this track progress, but it also informs future investment decisions, ensuring continuous alignment with personal values and strategic goals.

For financial planners and advisors assisting clients with these options, the path involves educating themselves thoroughly about both the risks and the rewards. Understanding regulatory environments, staying updated on industry trends, and having a network of vetted opportunities are crucial to making impactful recommendations. Furthermore, advisors must understand each client's unique definition of impact, tailoring strategies that meet both their financial and personal objectives, ultimately ensuring that their investment journey is both fulfilling and prosperous.

Investors should remember that impact and community investing is not a one-size-fits-all approach. It's a journey, one that evolves as personal circumstances, societal challenges, and market opportunities shift over time. The impact-focused investing landscape offers a myriad of options that enable investors to cast a wider net in terms of influence, improving lives, communities, and the planet while working towards financial success. Whether you're starting out or refining an existing strategy, there's room to grow, learn, and make a difference — one investment at a time.

Green Bonds and Renewable Energy Investments target dual benefits: financial returns and positive environmental impact. These investments are a compelling part of the sustainable investing landscape, offering a bridge for investors to directly fund projects that mitigate climate change and support the transition to a low-carbon economy. Green bonds provide the means to raise capital for environmentally beneficial projects, while renewable energy investments enable growth and innovation in cleaner energy technologies.

To begin with, green bonds are a class of fixed-income securities designed specifically to support climate-related or environmental projects. They are issued by a wide range of entities including governments, financial institutions, and corporations. The primary allure of green bonds lies in their dual promise: contributing to sustainable initiatives while offering steady returns. Investors looking for less volatile, income-generating assets that align with their values often find these bonds appealing. Moreover, green bonds are structured similarly to traditional bonds, making them familiar and accessible to a broad range of investors.

One of the most distinctive features of green bonds is the transparency they offer. Issuers typically promise regular updating on how the proceeds are being deployed and the environmental benefits achieved, providing a significant degree of accountability. This transparency is crucial because it helps investors ensure that their funds are making the intended impact. It also fosters trust and encourages more investors to consider this investment vehicle as a viable option for generating both financial and social returns.

As the demand for environmentally friendly investment options has surged, so too has the issuance of green bonds. In recent years, the market has witnessed remarkable growth, both in size and diversity. In addition to traditional project-based green bonds, there are now sustainability-linked bonds on offer, which are tied to companies' broader ESG performance. This diversity highlights the evolving nature of green finance as companies and investors alike become more attuned to the importance of environmental stewardship.

Part of the allure of renewable energy investments is the sector's rapidly growing potential. As the world shifts toward reducing carbon footprints, renewable energy has taken center stage, presenting both challenges and opportunities for investors. Solar, wind, hydroelectric, and geothermal energy projects have seen significant advancements, making them more cost-efficient and technologically sophisticated. Investing in these sectors often includes acquiring stocks in renewable energy companies, investing in mutual funds or ETFs focused on green technologies, or financing specific projects directly.

Renewable energy stocks have become a focal point for those wanting to combine financial success with environmental benefits. Many companies in the renewable sector enjoy robust growth prospects fueled by innovation and increasing government support for clean energy. These stocks can provide significant gains, but they can also be more volatile compared to traditional investments. Therefore, diversification is essential, not only within the renewable energy sector but across an entire investment portfolio.

Moreover, investors have a choice between established renewable players and emerging companies. Established companies might offer stability and steady returns, while newer firms represent the potential for substantial capital appreciation as they introduce innovative solutions to the market. Each choice underscores the importance of due diligence to understand each company's fundamentals, growth trajectory, and risk profile.

Investing in renewable energy ETFs can provide a diversified exposure to the sector. These ETFs bundle together a variety of clean energy companies, spreading risk and offering a sampling of the industry's performance without committing to a single company. This approach can appeal to investors who want to embrace the renewable energy trend without the hands-on management that individual stock picking entails.

Given the systemic importance of transitioning to renewable energy, many governments have introduced incentives to spur investments and innovations within this sector. Tax credits and subsidies aim to make renewable projects more financially appealing, reducing initial costs and boosting investment returns. These government-backed benefits make renewable energy investments even more attractive to ecologically conscious investors seeking favorable financial returns.

In addition to financial returns, investing in green bonds and renewable energy allows investors to consciously support the world's shift towards sustainability. These investments make it possible to participate directly in the global efforts to combat climate change, aligning personal beliefs with financial choices. This connection between values and dollars can inspire investors to maintain their commitment to sustainable investing, even when faced with the natural fluctuations of financial markets.

Overall, green bonds and renewable energy investments offer a powerful avenue for sustainable investing. They enable individual investors, financial advisors, and fund managers to align portfolios with a sustainable future while earning competitive returns. By understanding the dynamics, risk profiles, and opportunities within these sectors, investors not only contribute to positive environmental outcomes but also capitalize on the momentum of global sustainability initiatives. Whether you're managing a substantial portfolio or just starting with modest amounts, exploring green bonds and renewable energy can be both an intelligent and responsible investment choice.

Chapter 10:
The Role of Financial Advisors
in Sustainable Investing

As we dive into the pivotal role financial advisors play in sustainable investing, it's clear that they're not just about balancing risk and return; they're also gatekeepers of a new era of conscientious investing. These professionals are uniquely positioned to guide investors through the complex terrain of integrating environmental, social, and governance (ESG) criteria into portfolios. The challenge and opportunity lie in aligning financial goals with personal values, and advisors are critical in bridging this gap. By developing bespoke strategies that include sustainable investment options, advisors can help investors feel confident about their financial decisions and their ethical implications. Moreover, in a field that's constantly evolving, continuous education is essential for advisors to keep up with emerging trends and regulatory shifts. This ensures they're always equipped to provide cutting-edge advice tailored to both the current market landscape and an individual's specific sustainability goals. Advisors thus become invaluable allies in crafting a future where financial success and social responsibility go hand in hand.

Finding the Right Advisor for Your Sustainable Portfolio marks a pivotal junction in your journey of integrating principles of sustainability into your investment strategy. It's akin to finding a partner who not only understands your financial goals but also resonates with your values and ethical considerations. This alignment is crucial, as the realm of sustainable investing is as dynamic as it is complex.

First, consider what "sustainability" means to you. This reflection helps in communicating your expectations to a prospective advisor. For some, it might be about prioritizing environmental concerns; for others, it could mean focusing on social justice or ethical governance. Your understanding of sustainability directly influences the kind of advisor you'll need. A clear vision empowers you to seek out professionals who specialize in those areas and have a proven track record.

When you embark on the search for a financial advisor, take the time to research and vet potential candidates meticulously. Consider starting with referrals from trusted friends, family, or colleagues who share your investment philosophy. This can provide insights into the advisor's expertise and compatibility with your goals. Additionally, professional organizations, such as the Financial Planning Association, may offer directories of advisors who focus on sustainable investing.

Evaluation of a potential advisor's credentials is paramount. Look for certifications or designations like Chartered SRI Counselor (CSRIC) that indicate a commitment to sustainable investing education. Professional qualifications are important, but a personal alignment is equally crucial. An advisor should have a philosophy and moral compass that reflects your own, ensuring a cohesive strategy for achieving your financial objectives.

An interview or initial consultation with potential advisors can provide invaluable insights. This meeting is an opportunity to gauge their understanding of environmental, social, and governance (ESG) criteria and their practical application in investment strategies. Ask questions about their approach to integrating ESG factors into portfolios, their methodology for performing due diligence on sustainable investments, and how they handle changes in this fast-evolving field.

Transparency is another cornerstone when dealing with financial advisors. Ensure that any potential advisor is willing to disclose their fee structure upfront. Whether they work on a flat fee, hourly rate, or commission basis can significantly impact both your financial planning and the ongoing relationship. Understanding these details early helps avoid conflicts of interest and ensures that the advice you receive is genuinely in your best interest.

Communication is pivotal. Can your advisor explain complex financial concepts in simple terms? Do they make you feel heard and valued? These interpersonal skills are just as essential as technical proficiency. An advisor should not only amend your portfolio as necessary but also educate and guide you through the decision-making process, adapting to any changes in your life conditions or investment goals.

Moreover, consider the advisor's network and resources. An advisor who is actively engaged in the sustainable investment community is more likely to be up-to-date with the latest trends, tools, and opportunities. They should partake in ongoing learning, attend industry conferences, and contribute to thought leadership in the field, as sustainable investing is constantly evolving.

Technology can also play a significant role in your relationship with an advisor. Innovative advisors utilize fintech solutions and sustainable investment platforms to provide transparency and enhance the management of your portfolio. Robo-advising tools, for example, offer algorithm-driven recommendations, which can supplement the human touch of your advisor, making the process more robust and agile.

It's essential to revisit the advisor-client relationship periodically. Market conditions and personal circumstances can change, and your advisor should be proactive about suggesting adjustments to your portfolio that reflect both external factors and your internal priorities. Consistent reviews ensure that your sustainable portfolio remains aligned with your core values and financial goals.

In sum, finding the right advisor is not merely about choosing someone to manage your investments; it's about enlisting a strategic partner who will journey with you as you endeavor to align personal values with financial objectives. With the right advisor, the fusion of ethical values and financial acumen becomes a powerful tool for both wealth creation and doing good in the world.

Robo-Advisors and Sustainable Investment Platforms are playing an increasingly pivotal role in the landscape of sustainable investing. With technology reshaping how we interact with and manage our investments, robo-advisors have become a crucial tool for those who want to align their portfolios with their values. They're not just offering cost-effective solutions but also providing access to investment strategies that prioritize environmental, social, and governance (ESG) criteria.

Robo-advisors utilize sophisticated algorithms to create personalized investment portfolios. This level of customization allows investors to tailor their portfolios to their specific sustainable goals. These platforms analyze ESG data, ensuring investments meet certain sustainable criteria. They bring the opportunity for everyday investors to participate in sustainable investing without needing a deep understanding of financial markets or ESG factors.

One of the key benefits of using robo-advisors is their ability to democratize sustainable investing. Historically, sustainable investment options were limited to high-net-worth individuals or institutional investors. However, with robo-advisors, the barrier to entry has significantly reduced. These platforms offer low minimum investments and transparent fee structures, making sustainable investing accessible to a broader audience.

The technology behind robo-advisors also supports regular portfolio rebalancing, an essential aspect of maintaining a sustainable investment strategy. Through automated processes, these platforms can adjust and realign portfolios based on evolving ESG data, market conditions, and personal investment goals. This agility ensures sustainability-focused portfolios remain aligned with both market performance and investor values over time.

Moreover, robo-advisors offer the advantage of continuous monitoring and reporting. Investors receive regular updates and insights into how their investments align with their sustainable goals. This transparency builds trust and keeps investors informed about the impact of their portfolios. Seeing tangible results in terms of reduced carbon emissions or positive social impact can be incredibly motivational for investors dedicated to making a difference through their financial decisions.

On the other hand, sustainable investment platforms often partner with robo-advisors to enhance their offerings. These platforms provide detailed ESG data and analytics, which are crucial for informed decision-making. By integrating these resources, robo-advisors can enhance their portfolio strategies, offering clients opportunities to contribute to renewable energy projects or social enterprises actively. Thus, a synergy is created, combining automation with expert insight.

However, leveraging technology in sustainable investing isn't without its challenges. One of the primary concerns is ensuring that the ESG data utilized by robo-advisors is accurate and up-to-date. The quality of the data significantly impacts investment decisions and outcomes. Therefore, robust systems for data verification and validation are essential to maintain the integrity of sustainable investment portfolios.

Despite these challenges, the number of people adopting robo-advisors for sustainable investing continues to grow. The ease of use, coupled with the ability to set and forget investment strategies, is particularly appealing for younger investors. Millennials and Generation Z show a strong preference for investments that align with their personal beliefs and goals; robo-advisors offer a streamlined way to achieve this alignment without requiring extensive financial knowledge.

The emotional appeal of sustainable investing can't be underestimated. Knowing your investments are contributing to a better world adds an intangible value to the financial returns. Robo-advisors are making it easier for investors to feel confident about where their money is going and the impact it's making. As these platforms evolve, they are likely to incorporate more advanced features relating to impact measurement and reporting, providing even more robust tools for socially conscious investors.

Furthermore, the integration of artificial intelligence (AI) with robo-advisors is beginning to enhance their capability to assess complex ESG metrics. AI can process vast amounts of data, identifying trends and predicting future scenarios that help refine sustainable investment strategies. This technological advancement promises to make robo-advisors even more integral to the world of finance, especially as the demand for ESG investments continues to rise.

Overall, robo-advisors and sustainable investment platforms represent a transformative shift in how individuals approach investing. By bridging the gap between technology and sustainability, they provide an accessible path for those looking to integrate their values with their financial goals. As more investors recognize the importance of sustainability, the role of these platforms is set to grow even further, influencing not just individual portfolios, but the broader financial landscape.

In conclusion, the rise of robo-advisors in sustainable investing signifies a new era where technology meets purpose. They empower investors to take control of their financial futures in a way that's aligned with their values, providing tools and insights that were once only available to institutions or the wealthy. As the ESG investing trend continues to build momentum, robo-advisors and sustainable investment platforms will undoubtedly become essential components of a value-driven investment strategy.

The Importance of Ongoing Education for Advisors is vital in navigating the constantly evolving field of sustainable investing. Given the rapid pace at which new sustainable products and ESG criteria develop, financial advisors must continually update their knowledge and skills. New regulatory frameworks, technological advancements, and shifts in public policy mean that what worked yesterday may not be effective today. Advisors who embrace education and stay informed offer a significant value add to their clients who are concerned with making meaningful investments.

For advisors in sustainable investing, the learning never truly stops. New investment vehicles, such as green bonds and impact funds, are constantly being introduced. Navigating these options requires an acute awareness of their characteristics, benefits, and potential risks. Without ongoing education, advisors risk falling behind, unable to effectively serve their clients who trust them to offer sound and up-to-date advice.

A commitment to education ensures that advisors can meet regulatory requirements and industry standards, which are increasingly stringent in the realm of sustainable investments. Governments worldwide are introducing mandates for ESG disclosures, necessitating that advisors understand both the legal requirements and the ethical implications. Educated advisors will be better equipped to guide clients through these regulatory landscapes.

Moreover, continuous learning expands an advisor's ability to foster deeper client relationships. When advisors speak confidently and knowledgeably about the complexities of ESG factors or sustainable investment strategies, clients are more likely to feel secure in their investment choices. Education allows advisors to explain these often complex topics in relatable terms, bridging the gap between investment and impact goals. This capability is particularly crucial when serving a diverse audience, such as young professionals, retirees, or business owners, each bringing unique financial objectives.

Another facet of ongoing education is its role in advancing an advisor's professional reputation and credibility. In an industry where trust is paramount, advisors must demonstrate not only their competence but also their commitment to personal and professional growth. Attending workshops, earning certifications, or engaging in relevant webinars underscores their expertise and dedication to the practice of sustainable investing.

As sustainable investing is continuously shaped by global and local events, ongoing education also involves understanding geopolitical and economic factors that can affect ESG considerations. Advisors need to be aware of cultural shifts and technological innovations that might influence client interests and investment opportunities. This understanding helps them guide clients toward portfolios that not only yield financial returns but also align with the clients' values and social commitments.

Educational endeavors can also include collaborative learning and sharing insights with peers. Engagement in professional networks or attending conferences exposes advisors to new ideas and perspectives, promoting a culture of shared success. This collective knowledge and the mutual support gained are invaluable as advisors endeavor to tailor sustainable investment solutions to meet diverse client needs and aspirations.

Financial advisors are often tasked with demystifying complex subjects for their clients, making ongoing education even more critical. They need to stay updated on innovations in investment products and strategies to communicate these effectively to their clients. This means being able to translate technical jargon into understandable concepts that resonate with the investors' values and financial goals. The ability to educate clients also empowers them, enabling more informed decision-making, thus enhancing the advisor-client relationship.

Additionally, staying educated empowers advisors to challenge assumptions and evaluate investment strategies critically. With robust knowledge, they can discern between investments genuinely contributing to sustainability and those that are merely marketing green virtues—a task that has grown increasingly challenging with incidents of greenwashing. Here, education serves as a defense, helping advisors sift through information with a discerning eye and ultimately providing recommendations rooted in authenticity.

The pursuit of ongoing education involves various strategies and resources, from pursuing advanced courses to participating in industry-specific training programs or engaging with thought leaders in sustainable investing. Online platforms, books, and academia provide ample resources to stay ahead. By leveraging these, advisers can maintain a cutting edge that serves them and their clients well. Continuous learning is not merely a professional obligation but an opportunity for personal growth, reinforcing ethics and empathy required in designing and managing inclusive financial plans.

The influence of advisors extends beyond financial markets into broader societal impact, making their role indispensable in driving sustainable change. Equipped with updated knowledge, advisors can inspire confidence and commitment in their clients to pursue investments that stand the test of time, benefiting individual portfolios and society at large. In doing so, they don't just manage wealth; they help shape the future, stewarding a legacy of sustainability-driven decisions and values.

Ultimately, ongoing education strengthens the advisor's capacity to serve as a guide and a partner in the journey toward sustainable financial futures. It supports precise, informed, and strategic investment decisions while fostering a profound understanding of environmental, social, and governance realities. By continuously honing their expertise, advisors can more effectively align investment opportunities with the evolving goals and values of the clients they serve.

Chapter 11:
Measuring the Impact of Your Sustainable Investments

In the evolving world of sustainable investing, gauging the real-world impact of your choices is both a science and an art. With a mix of heart and data, you'll learn to navigate this landscape using practical tools and meaningful metrics that tell the story of your ESG investments. It's not just about championing shareholder advocacy or practicing active ownership; it's about realizing the power of your investments to initiate positive change. By engaging deeply with the companies you invest in, you not only ensure that your portfolio aligns with your principles but also leverage your influence to drive corporate behavior towards sustainability. This chapter illuminates the paths and strategies that will enable you to measure tangible outcomes, offering a roadmap to transforming your objectives into measurable impacts. So, let's delve into how you can assess and amplify the influence of your sustainable investment portfolio in pursuing not just financial returns but also a legacy of ethical contribution.

Tools and Metrics for Assessing ESG Performance play a critical role in understanding how effectively your sustainable investments are achieving the desired impact. As you delve deeper into measuring the success of your investments, it's essential to harness the right tools and employ metrics that accurately reflect environmental, social, and governance criteria. These tools not only provide clarity but also ensure that your investment decisions align with your values and long-term financial goals. They serve as a compass, guiding investors through the complex terrain of sustainable investing, ensuring that each step taken contributes to a more sustainable future.

ESG performance assessment starts with robust data. Third-party research providers such as MSCI, Sustainalytics, and Morningstar offer detailed analyses of companies' ESG credentials. These providers aggregate data from various sources, including company disclosures, regulatory filings, and media reports, to assess how well a company performs on ESG issues. By using these insights, investors can gauge potential risks and opportunities, ensuring their portfolios align with their sustainability objectives. This data-driven approach helps reduce the risk of greenwashing—where companies overstate their commitment to sustainability—which remains a significant concern for conscientious investors.

Metrics are fundamental in measuring ESG performance. They translate qualitative parts of ESG performance into quantifiable data, offering a clear picture of how companies are performing over time. Common metrics include carbon footprint measures, diversity ratios, and board independence percentages. For example, carbon footprint metrics can help investors determine a company's overall contribution to climate change and assess its efforts to reduce carbon emissions. By focusing on these metrics, investors can hold companies accountable and ensure they deliver on their sustainability promises.

To complement these metrics, ESG ratings provide a comprehensive evaluation of a company's ESG performance. These ratings range from A to D or similar scales, offering a snapshot of how well a company is managing its ESG responsibilities. Investors use these ratings to compare companies within the same sector and to make informed decisions about where to allocate their capital. It's important, however, to understand the methodology behind these ratings, as different rating agencies might weigh ESG factors differently. Therefore, cross-referencing ratings from multiple providers can offer a more balanced view.

The rise of technology has provided additional tools for ESG assessment, such as advanced analytics and artificial intelligence (AI) platforms. These technologies streamline massive data analysis, offering investors real-time insights into ESG trends and performance. AI-driven platforms can also predict future ESG risks by analyzing historical data patterns, allowing investors to take preemptive action when necessary. This predictive capability is particularly valuable in a rapidly changing world where new ESG issues can emerge suddenly and unpredictably.

Apart from technology, corporate engagement is another effective tool for assessing ESG performance. By actively engaging with companies, investors can influence corporate policies and practices, particularly in areas like environmental sustainability and social equity. Investors can attend shareholder meetings, vote on ESG-related proposals, or directly engage with management teams to express their concerns or support. This active ownership approach helps investors not only assess but also improve the ESG performance of their investments, driving tangible change within companies.

Impact dashboards have emerged as another powerful tool for assessing ESG performance. By offering visual representations of how investments fare across various ESG metrics, these dashboards help investors quickly identify strengths and areas for improvement within their portfolios. Such dashboards can be customized to align with an investor's specific values and objectives, ensuring they focus on the issues most important to them, be it climate impact or labor practices.

Scenario analysis and stress testing add another layer of assessment, helping investors understand how their portfolios might perform under various ESG-related scenarios, such as drastic climate policy shifts or social upheavals. These tools enable investors to assess the resilience of their portfolios, ensuring they are well-positioned to withstand significant ESG-related changes. Scenario analysis encourages proactive strategy adjustments, rather than reactive fixes, securing long-term investment success.

It's also crucial to integrate ESG assessments into the regular performance reviews of an investment portfolio. This ongoing evaluation ensures that ESG factors remain integral to investment decisions, rather than an afterthought. Continuous assessment allows investors to adapt to new insights or technologies and refine their strategies based on what's working and what isn't. Regular updates foster transparency, bolster investor confidence, and maintain alignment with sustainable financial goals.

While tools and metrics for assessing ESG performance can seem complex, breaking them down into practical steps makes them accessible for individual investors and families alike. Start by prioritizing the issues that matter most to your values and financial objectives. Choose data providers and metrics that align with these priorities and utilize technology to enhance your analysis. Engage directly with companies for a more nuanced view and leverage dashboards for easy visualization.

Remember, measuring ESG performance is a journey, not a destination. By continually refining the tools and metrics you use, you'll drive not just financial returns but also positive change in the world. This dual focus on profit and purpose ensures that your investments don't just secure your financial future but actively contribute to a more sustainable planet. Amidst all these considerations, becoming adept at using these tools will empower you to navigate the world of sustainable investing with confidence and clarity.

Shareholder Advocacy and Active Ownership is not just a strategy—it's a commitment. As responsible investors seek to blend financial returns with societal impact, shareholder advocacy becomes an invaluable tool in the sustainable investment toolkit. Unlike passive investors, active owners take the reins, leveraging their influence to drive corporate behavior change and promote transparency, accountability, and sustainability across industries.

The heart of shareholder advocacy lies in a straightforward yet powerful concept: using your stake in a company to push for positive change. It involves engaging with corporate management on critical issues related to environmental stewardship, social responsibility, and governance excellence. This isn't some abstract or niche activity; it's a vibrant, impactful practice reshaping our corporate landscapes and involving participants across various market sectors.

Engagement takes many forms, from direct dialogues with corporate executives to attending annual meetings where pressing issues are debated and voted on. But it doesn't stop there. Active ownership can also involve filing shareholder resolutions, which compel corporations to consider and publicly respond to pressing concerns raised by investors. Such resolutions, even when they don't win a majority vote, send a clear signal: shareholders are watching, and they'll keep the pressure on until meaningful changes occur.

One of the compelling aspects of shareholder advocacy is its potential to amplify collective power. By forming coalitions, individual investors can pool their resources, aligning efforts with like-minded shareholders to magnify their influence. This collaboration extends beyond individual interests; it's about creating waves of change that can alter corporate policies and practices on a broader scale, fostering a culture of responsibility and innovation.

Research shows that engaged shareholders can lead to tangible improvements in corporate ESG performance. Companies that listen and respond to their shareholders often witness enhanced brand reputation, mitigated risks, and, ultimately, stronger long-term performance. For investors committed to sustainable practices, active ownership isn't merely a strategy for optimizing investment returns; it's a catalyst for meaningful, systemic change.

This strategy of proactive engagement hinges on effective communication and a deep understanding of the issues at stake. Investors need to stay informed about global trends and local realities that impact their investments. Being aware of industry-specific challenges and opportunities allows shareholders to craft informed inquiries and articulate compelling arguments to corporate executives, fostering dialogue that can transform boardroom priorities.

Though engaging with companies can lead to significant changes, it's not without its challenges. Resistance from corporate management, especially in cases where proposed changes might disrupt immediate profitability, is not uncommon. Additionally, shareholders often navigate complex regulatory environments and must be prepared to deal with varying degrees of transparency and receptivity from the companies they engage with. This complex landscape requires persistence, patience, and a strategic mindset.

Despite these hurdles, the trend toward increased shareholder advocacy shows no signs of slowing down. Institutional investors, including pension funds and insurance companies, are increasingly joining forces with retail investors to apply pressure where it's needed most. This collective push aligns investors with companies that share their values, ensuring that businesses not only look good on paper but also commit to sustainable practices in action.

It's worth noting that technological advances are facilitating more effective shareholder advocacy. Digital platforms are making it easier for investors to collaborate, share insights, and mobilize efforts in real-time. The increased transparency afforded by digital tools also means that companies are more accountable to their shareholders—and to the public—than ever before.

But what's an investor to do to become an active owner and engage in shareholder advocacy effectively? It begins with education. Understanding both the power and responsibility of shareholder influence is crucial. Investors should explore resources, understand proxy voting guidelines, consider joining advocacy groups, and, importantly, not shy away from asking hard questions. Your voice matters. Your advocacy can create shifts not just within a single company but across markets and sectors.

Ultimately, shareholder advocacy is about creating alignment between personal values and corporate actions. The goal isn't to dictate corporate strategies but to encourage practices that lead to long-term value creation for shareholders and enduring benefits for society and the environment. By remaining engaged, informed, and proactive, investors can wield their power wisely, supporting businesses that contribute positively to the world.

Incorporating shareholder advocacy and active ownership into one's investment approach requires courage and discipline. It's not just about ethics and responsibility; it's about realizing that sustainable investing has the power to reimagine the future. Your investments— when actively managed with intent and purpose—can drive the necessary change, ensuring that businesses contribute positively to our shared environmental and social challenges.

As we delve deeper into sustainable investing, remember that your role as an investor extends beyond financial returns. Each dialogue facilitated, every resolution proposed, and each vote cast are opportunities to align corporate conduct with the shared goal of a sustainable future. Shareholder advocacy isn't just about wielding influence; it's about crafting a legacy. As you engage in this powerful practice, you'll be part of an evolving narrative where investments don't just grow wealth—they nourish the world.

Engaging with Companies for Positive Change involves leveraging your position as an investor to drive companies towards more sustainable practices. It's a crucial aspect of sustainable investing because it underscores the role investors can play in shaping corporate behaviors and policies. Whether you're a small shareholder or part of a large investment group, your voice matters. The concept here is active ownership, where investors don't just provide capital but also engage constructively with companies to promote better environmental, social, and governance (ESG) practices.

As investors, you have the opportunity to approach companies with the intention of fostering dialogue around sustainability. This engagement can take many forms, from voting on shareholder resolutions to participating in direct discussions with company management. Developing a robust engagement strategy means identifying the issues that matter most to you and your values, such as carbon emissions, human rights, or diversity and inclusion. With this focus, your efforts can be more targeted and impactful.

One of the powerful tools at your disposal is the proxy vote. Proxy voting allows shareholders to influence the corporate governance of companies in which they invest. By casting your vote on key policy decisions, you can advocate for changes that align with sustainable principles. However, meaningful engagement often goes beyond just voting. Entering into dialogues with companies either independently or collaboratively with other investors can generate significant pressure for change. Shareholder advocacy groups often facilitate these joint efforts, amplifying the voices of smaller investors and enhancing the impact of collective action.

Consider how you can utilize shareholder resolutions. These proposals submitted by shareholders to the company board request specific changes or actions. While particularly common in larger companies, where gathering the requisite support is realistic, even smaller-scale investors can effect change by aligning with larger coalition groups. These resolutions can address a variety of issues, from urging companies to establish targets for renewable energy use to demanding transparent reporting of greenhouse gas emissions. Although management may initially resist these motions, consistent and devoted shareholder engagement often leads to essential conversations on these topics.

While active engagement is about dialogue and persuasion, it sometimes requires a firmer stance. Investors may choose to divest as a last resort if companies remain unresponsive to sustainable demands. Divestment sends a strong signal but is often more effective when combined with proactive engagement strategies. Divesting isn't just a means to cleanse a portfolio ethically; it's a message to the market that unsustainable practices won't be financially rewarded.

Monitoring company performance on ESG metrics is key throughout this process. As an investor, your role includes understanding these metrics and using them to drive informed discussions with the companies you're engaging. These metrics should be clear and aligned with established benchmarks, like those from the Global Reporting Initiative (GRI) or the Sustainability Accounting Standards Board (SASB). Reviewing this data not only helps in assessing current performance but also in tracking improvements over time and holding companies accountable to their commitments.

Engagement requires patience and persistence. It's not uncommon for notable changes to emerge only after years of dialog and pressure. Consider the work of social change often achieved through sustained effort—corporate evolution towards sustainability mirrors this process. By continually revisiting dialogues, measuring outcomes, and applying pressure when necessary, investors can generate tangible outcomes. Regular updates with management, augmented by fact-based arguments and commitments to continued advocacy, can build the necessary momentum for lasting change.

For those who are relatively new to engaging with companies, collaborating with experienced advocacy groups can offer guidance and increase influence. Organizations like the Interfaith Center on Corporate Responsibility (ICCR) and Ceres facilitate cooperative activism, providing resources and platforms for smaller investors to join forces with others. These alliances can leverage greater change than any single entity might achieve alone.

It's also essential to remember that change isn't always linear or tension-free. Corporate leadership may initially resist, citing financial or operational challenges as reasons not to adopt proposed ESG improvements. For investors, this means being well-prepared with research and arguments that highlight the long-term benefits and mitigate fears surrounding initial costs or disruptions. In many cases, sustainable practices lead to improved profitability and brand reputation over time.

Finally, celebrate your wins and learn from setbacks. Not all engagements will succeed, but each interaction is an opportunity to refine your approach, gather insights, and strengthen future efforts. Successful advocacy stories should be shared and used as blueprints for other endeavors, while less successful campaigns can foster alternative strategies and cohesion among like-minded investors.

Engaging with companies for positive change isn't just an obligation—it's an opportunity. The drive towards a sustainable future requires investors who are willing to commit their financial capital and influence towards promoting responsible corporate behavior. By combining your financial objectives with active engagement strategies, you can play a vital role in steering the corporate world towards more sustainable outcomes. This journey calls not only for informed strategy but also for determination, resilience, and the belief that individual actions, galvanized through collective will, have the potential to create a more sustainable and equitable global market.

105

Chapter 12:
Overcoming Challenges in Sustainable Investing

Embarking on the journey of sustainable investing isn't just about aligning financial goals with personal values—it's also about navigating a complex landscape filled with challenges. As the field evolves, investors confront issues like greenwashing, where companies exaggerate their environmental efforts, making it crucial to stay vigilant and informed. Keeping abreast of ESG trends and regulatory changes is equally important in a rapidly shifting environment. To make a profound impact, engaging in advocacy and policy discussions can amplify the reach of sustainable initiatives, propelling change on a larger scale. Strategic alliances with knowledgeable advisors can further fortify these efforts, ensuring your investments not only thrive but also drive meaningful societal and environmental outcomes. By tackling these hurdles head-on, the path to creating a sustainable legacy becomes clearer and more attainable.

Addressing Greenwashing and Other Concerns is a critical issue in the realm of sustainable investing. As more investors show interest in aligning their portfolios with their values, the financial markets have responded with a plethora of new ESG products. However, this rapid expansion has given rise to "greenwashing," where companies exaggerate or fabricate their sustainability efforts to appeal to conscious investors. The challenge is separating fact from fiction and ensuring that investments truly make a positive impact.

Investors often find themselves questioning the authenticity of a company's ESG claims. This skepticism is, unfortunately, justified as cases of greenwashing continue to emerge, casting doubt on the legitimacy of sustainable finance initiatives. To tackle this, investors need to employ due diligence and deep dive into the methodologies that firms use to report their ESG metrics. Understanding the framework and standards such as the GRI (Global Reporting Initiative) and SASB (Sustainability Accounting Standards Board) can offer some assurance, though it's important to remember that no standard is foolproof.

Moreover, transparency is key. Encouraging and advocating for clear and honest communication from companies about their sustainability practices can help mitigate the risks associated with greenwashing. Shareholder engagement plays a pivotal role in demanding better disclosures. By actively participating in annual meetings or exercising voting rights, investors can press for greater accountability and change. It's not just about avoiding deceptive practices; it's about setting higher standards for what constitutes a sustainable investment.

The rise of third-party ESG data providers has also been instrumental in combating greenwashing. These organizations use rigorous criteria to evaluate a company's ESG performance, offering investors an additional layer of verification. However, reliance on these sources requires an understanding of potential biases or limitations in their data collection processes. Smart investors will compare multiple data sources to get a comprehensive view of a potential investment.

Understanding the difference between intentional and unintentional greenwashing can be crucial. Some companies may inadvertently mislead investors due to poor data integrity or inadequate reporting processes. In these cases, investor engagement can help identify these gaps and encourage companies to improve their practices. Continuous dialogue between companies and their investors will not only reduce the chances of greenwashing but also foster a more collaborative approach to sustainable business practices.

In addition to discerning between greenwashed and genuine ESG investments, the conversation around sustainability must also address broader concerns such as financial performance and regulatory compliance. Investors often worry that sustainable investing may compromise returns. However, numerous studies have begun to show that companies with strong ESG practices often exhibit less volatility and demonstrate resilience during market downturns, debunking the myth of inferior financial performance.

The regulatory landscape is evolving, with governments and industry bodies recognizing the importance of standardizing ESG reporting. Initiatives like the EU's Sustainable Finance Disclosure Regulation (SFDR) aim to enhance transparency and accountability, which can help in reducing greenwashing incidents. Keeping abreast of these regulations and understanding how they impact investment choices can arm investors with the knowledge needed to make informed decisions.

Addressing these concerns means that both investors and financial advisors must commit to ongoing education. As sustainable investing frameworks evolve, so too must our understanding. Financial planners who stay informed about the latest developments can better guide their clients through the complexities of this investment landscape, emphasizing both financial returns and impact.

Ultimately, the fight against greenwashing requires both vigilance and education. By cultivating a community of informed investors who are conscious of greenwashing risks and prepared to confront them, we can drive change. Responsible investors aren't just passive participants in the market; they're catalysts for change that hold companies accountable and push for sustainable practices.

Finally, it's crucial to remember that sustainable investing is a journey, not a destination. As more companies truly embrace their ESG responsibilities, the issue of greenwashing may become less prevalent. Until then, maintaining an informed, proactive approach will help investors navigate these challenges and ensure their portfolios make the impact intended. Together, we can move towards an investment environment where sustainable claims are not just marketing cliches, but genuine commitments to positive change.

Staying Informed in a Rapidly Evolving Landscape Sustainable investing has grown into a dynamic field that demands constant attention and responsiveness from investors. As with any burgeoning movement, the landscape is characterized by swift advancements and changes that can be both daunting and exciting. Investors committed to sustainable choices are not only engaging with financial data but also keeping tabs on social trends, environmental advances, and policy shifts that shape the markets. This section aims to impart strategies for investors to stay current amidst these evolving dynamics, ensuring informed decision-making as integral to their investing philosophy.

The very fabric of sustainable investing is woven from the threads of environmental, social, and governance (ESG) considerations, which themselves are in a state of continual evolution. Therefore, staying informed requires a multi-pronged approach. Firstly, there is the need for a robust framework for absorbing information. Investors should prioritize reliable sources like reputable financial news outlets, specialized ESG publications, and insights from seasoned analysts known for their understanding of sustainable practices. Subscribing to newsletters and alerts from ESG-focused entities can also provide timely updates and expert opinions.

Yet, the abundance of information available can lead to overwhelm. It's crucial, then, to develop the skill to discern value amidst this flood. Evaluate the credibility of each source, and weigh its perspectives against other inputs to establish an informed view of the current landscape. More than passively consuming information, engage with it critically—mindful of potential biases and the broader implications on your investment strategy. Ask yourself: Does this new development align with my chosen impact goals? What are the potential risks and opportunities presented by this shift?

Investors should make active use of technology to streamline this information-gathering process. Tools like customizable news aggregators and AI-driven platforms can help tailor and prioritize information that matches specific investing interests. For instance, you might set up alerts for reports on renewable energy advancements or shifts in corporate governance policies. These tools do more than save time; they help minimize the noise and focus on what truly matters for your portfolio.

Networking is another dimension that significantly contributes to staying informed. Engaging with other investors, attending conferences, and participating in webinars can expose you to diverse perspectives and insights. The value of validated sharing and receiving of knowledge cannot be understated. If feasible, join groups or forums dedicated to sustainable investing, creating a community of practice where you can share experiences and strategies with peers. This collaborative approach can uncover emerging trends that might not yet be on your radar, offering a competitive edge in navigating the landscape.

While automated tools and networks aid information processing, continuous education remains the cornerstone of staying relevant. Pursuing certification programs or attending workshops in sustainable finance can significantly bolster your understanding of complex ESG metrics and how they apply to your portfolio. As regulations and frameworks evolve—think European Union's Sustainable Finance

Disclosure Regulation (SFDR) or updates in the Global Reporting Initiative (GRI)—it is beneficial for investors to have foundational knowledge that allows them to quickly comprehend and adapt to these changes.

Policy and regulatory changes also shape the sustainable investing landscape in profound ways. Therefore, maintaining an awareness of policy developments is essential. This might involve monitoring governmental and regulatory announcements or consulting experts who specialize in these areas. Changes in legislation or policy can present substantial risks or opportunities; understanding the direction policy is heading allows you to better anticipate and adjust your strategies accordingly.

Moreover, consider that sustainable investing is not a journey you undertake alone. Financial advisors and planners who specialize in this field can be invaluable resources in providing tailored advice based on the latest developments. Choosing an advisor with a proven track record in ESG can enhance your strategy's effectiveness and keep your portfolio aligned with the evolving best practices and opportunities in the market.

In this rapidly evolving landscape, adaptability and resilience are key. Be prepared to iterate on your strategies as new innovations and challenges arise. The shifts in technology, regulation, and market expectations surrounding sustainable investing are unlikely to slow down. But this dynamic environment also presents unparalleled opportunities to make impactful contributions through your investments, aligning your portfolio with values that reflect more than just financial return.

Finally, remember that while staying informed is a continuous process, it is also a rewarding one. As you invest time and resources into understanding this evolving landscape, you are not only safeguarding your portfolio but also enhancing the impact your investments have on the world. Your dedication to staying current positions you as a leader in the conscious investing community, capable of influencing meaningful change and inspiring others along the path of sustainable financial growth.

In conclusion, maintaining a well-rounded, adaptable approach to information gathering in the face of rapid evolution is vital for sustainable investors. As you carve out your path, allow curiosity and commitment to guide your investment journey. Balance keeping pace with the dynamic environment while holding firm to the values and impact goals that shape your vision—embarking on this continuous learning process not just as a duty, but as a mission that resonates with purpose and passion.

Advocacy and Policy Engagement for Broader Impact is a powerful lever in overcoming challenges in sustainable investing. While individual actions matter, collective advocacy can amplify the impact of these efforts. Leveraging advocacy goes beyond simply investing in companies that align with your values; it involves actively engaging with policymakers, businesses, and communities to create systemic change.

Sustainable investing is not just about aligning investments with personal values but also about influencing the broader financial ecosystem. Advocacy becomes crucial in championing policies that facilitate the expansion and depth of sustainable practices within industries and sectors. For individual investors and advisors alike, participating in advocacy provides an avenue to express their values and drive tangible changes within financial systems and the regulatory landscape.

Engaging in policy advocacy might sound daunting at first, particularly to those new to sustainable investing, yet it can start with simple, practical steps. Knowledge is power. The first step in advocacy is understanding the legislative landscape—knowing what policies are in place and where gaps exist. Initiatives like tax incentives for green projects or regulations penalizing high-carbon footprints are examples where investors can push for policies that level the playing field for sustainable practices.

Policy advocacy is not limited to high-level lobbying. Everyday investors can participate through grassroots efforts, such as signing petitions, supporting campaigns, or joining organizations focused on sustainable finance transformation. These group efforts often have a powerful collective impact. They draw attention to essential issues and bring critical mass to support needed changes. Your voice, as part of a larger chorus, can be a significant factor in driving innovation and fostering sustainable development.

Corporate policy engagement should also be considered. Financial planners and wealth managers can work with companies to establish and promote governance practices that prioritize sustainability. This includes advocating for transparency in reporting, regular ESG performance reviews, and sustainable practices embedded in corporate strategy. Advisors can guide companies in adopting frameworks that align with sustainable investment principles, ensuring that corporations not only follow regulations but also lead in setting new standards.

Furthermore, direct shareholder advocacy is a powerful tool that can drive change from within the companies themselves. Investors can file shareholder resolutions that require companies to address ESG concerns or to alter their operational strategies to align better with sustainability goals. Activist investors have the potential to push firms towards greater environmental responsibility and social fairness, promoting robust governance models that consider long-term impacts.

The effectiveness of advocacy and policy engagement frequently involves collaborative efforts with non-profit groups or international organizations. Partnerships with entities like the United Nations

Principles for Responsible Investment (UN PRI) or collaborating on industry initiatives can bolster the authority and reach of advocacy actions. These collaborations often provide investors with resources, data, and frameworks necessary to propose informed, impactful changes.

Influencing policy also includes engaging with regulators and government bodies tasked with overseeing markets and establishing public policy. Communicating the importance of integrating ESG considerations into mainstream financial regulation can guide policy development and foster an environment conducive to sustainable growth. Key areas of focus often include climate risk disclosure, facilitating responsible investment flows, and integrating sustainability into fiduciary duty.

Access to information and corporate transparency are cornerstones for investors wanting to enact change. Advocating for standardized, comprehensive ESG reporting ensures that investors can make decisions based on consistent and comparable data. Pressuring for policy changes that mandate such disclosures can significantly influence the industry's evolution towards transparency.

As we look to the future, the landscape of sustainable investing will undoubtedly continue to evolve. New challenges and opportunities will arise, requiring investors and advisors to remain nimble and proactive in their advocacy efforts. Staying informed, adapting to changes, and participating in dialogues with stakeholders including policymakers and corporate executives will ensure sustainable investing remains relevant and progressive.

In conclusion, the role of advocacy and policy engagement in sustainable investing cannot be overstated. It is a mechanism through which the financial industry can transcend individual action, addressing challenges such as greenwashing and enabling accountable growth across economic sectors. By leveraging collective influence, investors contribute to shaping a resilient and sustainable financial system for future generations.

Online Review Request for This Book We sincerely hope "Overcoming Challenges in Sustainable Investing" has equipped you with valuable insights and practical tools, and we'd be grateful if you could share your thoughts in an online review to help others benefit from this comprehensive guide.

The Future of Investing—Carrying Forward Your Sustainable Legacy

As we draw the curtains on our exploration of sustainable investing, it's important to reflect on the path we've charted and look forward to what lies ahead. Our journey began by aligning personal values with financial aspirations, laying the groundwork for impactful investing. Now, the future beckons, full of potential and promise, where financial growth harmonizes with ethical stewardship—truly a legacy worth carrying forward.

Imagine a future where your investments not only secure your financial well-being but also shape a more sustainable world. This isn't just a vision; it's a tangible opportunity. With every investment choice, you pave a path for equitable growth. By committing to sustainable practices, you're building an estate that transcends mere monetary value, creating ripples of positive change for generations to come. As you tread this path, embrace the complexities of ESG criteria and the nuances of asset allocation as tools that can unlock enduring impact.

Changing mindsets and embracing innovation can open doors to previously unimaginable outcomes. Consider how emerging technology intersects with sustainable investing. As digital platforms evolve, they provide unprecedented access to green investment options and ESG metrics. The financial landscape continues to shift, and with it, the rules of engagement. Staying ahead requires a proactive stance—continually learning, adapting, and seizing new opportunities that align with your values and financial goals.

The role of education can't be overstated. Whether you're a seasoned investor or just starting, understanding the intricacies of sustainable investing is vital. Entry points into sustainable markets have broadened, enabling more people to contribute. For the uninitiated, there are advisors and platforms dedicated to nurturing your ambitions, ensuring you wield the power to make informed choices. As this wave of conscientious investing gathers momentum, it pushes the boundaries of traditional finance, making sustainable investing accessible to all.

We mustn't overlook the role of policy and advocacy in shaping the future of investing. Transformative change often requires more than individual effort. It's about collective action—engaging with companies, governments, and other stakeholders to encourage transparency and enact meaningful policy changes. By advocating for robust ESG reporting standards and supporting environmentally forward-thinking legislation, you not only protect your investments but also contribute to a global shift towards sustainability.

The conversation around sustainable investing is far from static; it's a dynamically evolving field. As issues like climate change and social justice dominate headlines, more investors recognize the importance of integrating these factors into their portfolios. This evolution is driven by increasing awareness and a pressing need for solutions that are both profitable and socially responsible. By staying informed and adaptable, you can harness these developments, turning challenges into opportunities to reinforce your sustainable legacy.

Creating a sustainable legacy is about more than investments; it's about weaving sustainability into the very fabric of your life and the lives of those you influence. Generational financial education becomes crucial here. Teaching younger generations the importance of ethical investing instills values that endure long after we're gone. This legacy guides them in making choices that contribute positively to their communities and the world at large.

Looking ahead, philanthropy serves as a beacon, lighting pathways to impactful change. As discussed, integrating philanthropy into your investment strategy not only enriches your portfolio but also strengthens your legacy of giving. By leveraging financial instruments to support causes you care about deeply, you amplify the impact of your investments tenfold. The relationship between giving and investing becomes symbiotic, each enhancing the other to sustain a cycle of perpetual benefit.

As you embark on the future of investing, remember the central themes we've explored: aligning financial strategies with personal values, employing rigorous due diligence, and leveraging the expertise of advisors. It's about making informed decisions that transcend financial gain, echoing through time as a testament to mindful stewardship. The foundations you lay now will support a lasting and meaningful legacy.

In conclusion, the time is ripe for fostering a future where financial prosperity and sustainability coexist harmoniously. We've journeyed through the foundational aspects of sustainable investing, peered into advanced strategies, and explored the profound impact of our choices. Now, it's your turn to carry this knowledge forward. You'll find that investing in your values isn't just worthwhile; it's transformative. As you carry forward your sustainable legacy, remember that the seeds you plant today will blossom into a future where financial success and global sustainability thrive hand in hand.

Appendix A:
Resources for the Conscious Investor

The journey toward sustainable investing isn't one you have to take alone. A wealth of resources is at your disposal, offering insights, guidance, and tools to help align your investments with your values. Here's a curated list to support your path as a conscious investor.

Books and Publications

- **The Responsible Investor Handbook:** A comprehensive guide to sustainable and responsible investing strategies.

- **Investing in a Sustainable World:** This book provides a deep dive into the global trends influencing ESG investments.

- **Green to Gold:** Focused on sustainability in business, it offers insights valuable to investors seeking environmentally friendly options.

Online Platforms and Tools

- **ESG Rating Agencies:** Tools like MSCI ESG Ratings and Sustainalytics provide detailed analyses of companies' ESG performance.

- **Investment Platforms:** Platforms such as Swell Investing and Aspiration offer user-friendly interfaces and pre-selected ESG portfolios.

- **Carbon Footprint Calculators:** Tools like The Nature Conservancy's calculator can help assess the environmental impact of your investments.

Educational Websites

- **The Forum for Sustainable and Responsible Investment (US SIF):** Offers resources and research focused on sustainable investing.

- **Impact Investing Network (GIIN):** Provides a broad range of educational articles and guides on impact investing globally.

- **Principles for Responsible Investment (PRI):** Offers reports and guidance on ESG investing practices.

Podcasts and Videos

- **Impact Alpha:** A podcast dedicated to strategies for impact investors.

- **ESG Now:** This podcast provides insights into the latest trends in ESG investing.

- **Ted Talks on Sustainable Finance:** Offers innovative ideas and discussions on the role of finance in sustainability efforts.

Professional Organizations and Networks

- **Social Investment Forum (SIF):** Connects investors with sustainable investment opportunities.

- **Network for Sustainable Financial Markets (NSFM):** An international network aimed at facilitating discussions to advance sustainable financial markets.

- **Local Impact Investment Networks:** Many regions have investment networks focused on local sustainable investments.

Diving into conscious investing requires conviction, curiosity, and continuous learning. These resources aim to bolster your knowledge and decision-making skills, ensuring that your investments reflect your personal values and contribute positively to the world. Embrace the journey with confidence, equipped with the tools that empower strategic and impactful investing.

Glossary
of Sustainable Investing Terms

This glossary provides definitions for key terms associated with sustainable investing, helping you navigate the evolving landscape of ethical finance with confidence and clarity.

Active Ownership

The practice of investors engaging with companies to influence their practices and decisions, especially in relation to ESG (Environmental, Social, and Governance) issues. This can include voting at shareholder meetings and direct dialogue with company management.

Best-in-Class Investing

An investment approach where funds are allocated to companies within a particular industry or sector that lead in terms of ESG performance, rather than excluding entire industries.

Carbon Footprint

The total amount of greenhouse gases produced directly and indirectly by activities of an individual, organization, or product, usually expressed in equivalent tons of carbon dioxide (CO_2e).

Corporate Social Responsibility (CSR)

A self-regulating business model where companies integrate social and environmental concerns in their operations and interactions with stakeholders. It goes beyond profit and aims to positively impact society.

Divestment

The process of selling off investment from sectors or companies that are deemed unethical or non-sustainable, often used as a strategy to apply pressure on businesses to adopt more sustainable practices.

Environmental, Social, and Governance (ESG) Criteria

A set of standards for a company's behavior used by socially conscious investors to screen potential investments. They focus on environmentally sustainable practices, social impacts, and governance issues like corporate leadership and transparency.

Green Bonds

Debt securities issued to raise capital for projects that have positive environmental benefits. These projects might include renewable energy, energy efficiency, clean transportation, or sustainable water management.

Impact Investing

Investing with the intention to generate positive, measurable social and environmental impact alongside a financial return. This approach often targets pressing issues such as renewable energy, affordable housing, and healthcare.

Negative Screening

An investment strategy that excludes certain companies or industries from a portfolio based on specific criteria, often aligned with ethical or moral beliefs, such as tobacco, fossil fuels, or firearms.

Positive Screening

A strategy of including only those companies that meet certain criteria of sustainability or ethical performance into the investment portfolio, favoring those that actively contribute to a positive social or environmental impact.

Shareholder Advocacy

The use of shareholder power to influence corporate behavior by filing resolutions or participating in dialogues with companies on ESG issues.

Sustainable Development Goals (SDGs)

A collection of 17 global goals set by the United Nations General Assembly in 2015, aimed at ending poverty, protecting the planet, and ensuring prosperity for all by 2030.

Triple Bottom Line

An accounting framework with three parts: social, environmental, and financial. This framework suggests that companies commit to focus on social and environmental concerns just as they do on profits.

This glossary serves as a starting point for understanding the language and concepts that drive sustainable investing. By integrating these terms into your financial planning, you're not just investing for a return—you're contributing to a sustainable future.

Appendix B:
ESG Reporting Standards and Frameworks

As financial markets evolve and the urgency of sustainability grows, understanding ESG reporting standards and frameworks becomes crucial for anyone committed to responsible investing. These guidelines not only enhance transparency but also accentuate the alignment of investments with broader societal goals. Let's explore what they are, why they matter, and how you can use them to enrich your investment strategies.

The Purpose of ESG Reporting Standards

ESG reporting standards serve as the compass for companies and investors alike, guiding them towards responsible environmental, social, and governance practices. They aim to reflect the true impact of business activities beyond financial metrics. For investors, these standards translate into clear, comparable, and actionable insights that drive decision-making in alignment with personal values and broader ethical imperatives.

Key ESG Reporting Frameworks

- **Global Reporting Initiative (GRI):** As one of the most widely accepted frameworks, GRI sets a robust standard for sustainability reporting. It offers a comprehensive set of guidelines that help businesses communicate their economic, environmental, and social impacts effectively.

- **United Nations Global Compact (UNGC):** This framework encourages companies to adopt sustainable and socially responsible policies and to report on their implementation. It is built on ten principles covering human rights, labor, the environment, and anti-corruption.

- **Task Force on Climate-Related Financial Disclosures (TCFD):** Focusing primarily on climate-related risks, TCFD provides recommendations on the type of information companies should disclose to support informed decision-making by investors and stakeholders.

- **Sustainability Accounting Standards Board (SASB):** SASB standards target financial materiality and offer industry-specific guidelines for sustainability disclosure, enabling investors to assess ESG risks and opportunities across different sectors.

The Importance of Reliable ESG Data

High-quality ESG data forms the backbone of responsible investment practices. Without reliable data, assessing the sustainability performance of an investment becomes challenging and fraught with uncertainty. Companies are increasingly held accountable for providing accurate and verifiable ESG information, thus enhancing their credibility and appeal to conscientious investors.

Integrating ESG Frameworks into Investment Strategies

For investors, integrating ESG frameworks into their portfolio provides a structured approach to aligning investments with personal values and societal needs. By adopting these frameworks, investors not only refine their analysis but also amplify their influence in promoting sustainable practices across industries.

1. **Analyze ESG Reports:** Examine the ESG reports of potential investments using established frameworks to gauge their commitment and effectiveness in addressing key issues.

2. **Engage with Companies:** Use these insights to engage with companies, advocating for improved practices and transparency.

3. **Measure Impact:** Develop metrics to assess and monitor the real-world impact of investments, ensuring they meet personal and societal goals.

Investors who harness the power of ESG reporting standards become informed agents of change, equipped to create a ripple effect that extends far beyond their portfolios. By understanding and utilizing these frameworks, one lays the groundwork for a sustainable legacy that benefits not only oneself but also the world at large.

www.ingramcontent.com/pod-product-compliance
Lightning Source LLC
Chambersburg PA
CBHW030527210326
41597CB00013B/1050